Treasure of Fatima

Father Andrew Apostoli, C.F. R.

World Apostolate of Fatima, USA
Blue Army, USA
Washington, New Jersey
www.bluearmy.com   (866) 513-1917

First Printing, 2006

Photos from
©World Apostolate of Fatima, USA/Blue Army,USA

Scripture references from
The New American Bible ©Catholic Book Publishing Co.
unless otherwise noted

Printed in the United States of America
ISBN 0-9776504-0-5

AUTHOR'S PREFACE

Many people today have little or no understanding of the importance of the message given to the world by Our Blessed Lady at Fatima, Portugal, in 1917. She appeared on the 13th of every month from May to October of that year to three little shepherd children: Lucia Dos Santos, Francisco Marto and his sister Jacinta. Our Lady came with a message that was extremely important for the future of the world and its hope for peace. The Catholic Church recognizes that God the Father sent the Blessed Mother to these three shepherd children, and has accepted both the apparitions and the message given.

Today it is essential for the peace of the world that we respond to Our Lady's requests as fully as we can. Our Lady had warned that World War II would happen and Russia would spread the errors of Communism throughout the world if we did not heed her message. Since these evils did occur, we can only conclude that people did not respond as they should to the pleas of our Heavenly Mother. She said that she would come again at a later time to ask for the consecration of Russia to her Immaculate Heart and the Five First Saturdays Devotion.

On March 25, 1984 Pope John Paul II, in spiritual union with the bishops of the world, consecrated the world and Russia to the Immaculate Heart of Mary. Sister Lucia Dos Santos, the only remaining Fatima visionary, declared that Heaven accepted this consecration. What remains for us, now more than ever, is to carry out Our Lady's request for the special First Saturday Devotion.

We live in a time of great crisis in the world and even struggle within the Church. This present booklet is being offered as a means to help all our Catholic people respond with a better understanding and deeper love to what Our Lady has requested. Our Lady, herself, assures us that this devotion plays a significant part in her promise of the ultimate triumph of her Immaculate Heart. Please respond to Our Lady's request.

Fr. Andrew Apostoli, C.F.R.
August 11, 2005
Feast of Saint Clare of Assisi

CHAPTER 1

A Treasure From Fatima: The Five First Saturdays Devotion

One of the most important aspects of Our Lady of Fatima's message was her request for the devotion we call the "Five First Saturdays." I remember as a young boy how many people practiced this devotion in honor of Our Lady on the First Saturdays of five consecutive months. It seemed to be the natural complement to the Nine First Fridays' devotion in honor of the Sacred Heart of Jesus. Our Lord Himself had requested the First Friday devotion at the time of His apparitions to St. Margaret Mary Alacoque in the Visitation Monastery in Paray-le-Monial in France, during which He revealed the overwhelming love of His Sacred Heart for all of us. It was to be a devotion of prayer and reparation for those who offend His infinite love either by hatred, neglect or indifference.

The First Saturday devotion is also meant to be a devotion of prayer and reparation, specifically for those who offend against the Immaculate Heart of Our Lady. When I practiced this devotion as a young boy (and I still practice it today), I did not realize its beauty and depth. It was only years later that I learned that each of the Five First Saturdays was to be offered in reparation for very specific offenses against the Immaculate Heart of Our Lady. I wonder today how many Catholics even know of the devotion of the Five First Saturdays because it does not seem to be widely encouraged. Furthermore, I wonder how many of the people who do practice this devotion actually realize the historical background of this devotion. In subsequent chapters, I will offer reflections on the meaning of the reparation called for on each of the Five First Saturdays.

Our Lady Reveals Her Intention at Fatima

When Our Blessed Mother appeared to Lucia, Francisco and Jacinta on July 13, 1917, she confided the main part of her message to the children. They saw a most frightening vision of Hell, where there were both demons and lost souls in terrifying torment and despair. The young visionaries were completely shaken by the vision. Then Our Lady spoke kindly but sadly to them: "You have seen Hell where the souls of poor sinners go. To save them, God wishes to establish in the world devotion to my Immaculate Heart. If what I say to you is done, many souls will be saved and there will be peace." (Lucia's 4th Memoir)

Our Lady's message was focused on the salvation of souls, and specifically on her Immaculate Heart as God's chosen instrument to bring this about.

As Our Lady continued speaking, she revealed to the children that World War I, then raging, would come to an end. But she warned that a worse war, along with famine and persecution of the Church, especially of the Holy Father, would come about if people did not cease offending God. Then she added in her great maternal love for us: "To prevent this, I shall come to ask for the consecration of Russia to my Immaculate Heart, and the Communion of Reparation on the First Saturdays. If my requests are heeded, Russia will be converted, and there will be peace; if not, she will spread her errors throughout the world, causing wars and persecutions of the Church. The good will be martyred, the Holy Father will have much to suffer, various nations will be annihilated…" We have seen all of these unfortunate evils occur in the world in the 20th century!

Our Lady did add a message of hope when she said, "In the end, my Immaculate Heart will triumph. The Holy Father will consecrate Russia to me, and she will be converted, and a period of peace will be granted to the world." Ever since Pope John Paul II made the collegial consecration requested by Our Lady of Fatima on March 25, 1984, we have begun to see the conversion of Russia back to God, and "a period of peace" beginning to come upon the world. But more must yet be done, and this is where the devotion of the Five First Saturdays plays a vital role.

3

Our Lady Keeps Her Promise

Our Lady had said to the young visionaries, "I will come (again) to ask for...the Communion of Reparation on the First Saturdays..." Our Lady kept her promise on December 10, 1925. Francisco and Jacinta had already been taken to Heaven. Lucia, the remaining visionary of Fatima, was a postulant for the Dorothean Sisters at a convent in Pontevedra, Spain. Our Lady appeared to Lucia together with the Child Jesus. He spoke first to Lucia: "Have compassion on the Heart of your most holy mother, covered with thorns with which ungrateful men pierce it at every moment and there is no one who does an act of reparation to remove them." We know that all sin ultimately offends God, and so every act of reparation is ultimately directed to Him, to restore His earthly honor and glory that sin has offended and diminished. However, here Our Lord Himself extends the spirit of reparation, to restore the honor of the Immaculate Heart of His Blessed Mother, that sins directly against her have dishonored and diminished. How powerful are the words of His own request: "Have compassion on the Heart of your most holy mother!"

Then Our Lady, showing her Heart to Lucia, spoke, announcing her request: "Look, my daughter, at my Heart, surrounded with thorns with which ungrateful men pierce me at every moment by their blasphemies and ingratitude. You, at least; try to console me and say that I promise to assist at the hour of death, with the graces necessary for salvation, all

4

those who on the first Saturday of five consecutive months shall confess, receive Holy Communion, recite five decades of the Rosary, and keep me company for fifteen minutes while meditating on the 15 mysteries of the Rosary, with the intention of making reparation to me."

What a magnificent promise of Our Lady: that she would assist us with the graces needed for salvation at the most important moment of our lives – the moment of our death! Do we not pray to her for this every time we pray the Hail Mary: "Holy Mary, Mother of God, pray for us sinners, now and at the hour of our death"?

Our Lady states what is required to obtain her promise by practicing the First Saturday devotion. We can summarize these requirements into six points: (1) go to Confession (usually within the week before or after the First Saturday), (2) receive Holy Communion on the First Saturday itself, (3) recite five decades of the Rosary, (4) meditate on one or more of the Mysteries of the Rosary for an additional 15 minutes, (5) do all of these things with the intention of making reparation to the Immaculate Heart of Mary and (6) do these things on the First Saturday of five consecutive months.

In carrying out the 15-minute meditation/ conversation with Our Lady, each person should feel free to follow his or her own individual way of meditating. Furthermore, an individual can focus on one or more of the Rosary mysteries. However, it has been suggested that meditating on one mystery each month is the simplist way to fulfill this part of Our Lady's request.

To complete our understanding of the devotion of reparation on the Five First Saturdays, it is important to know why there are five times of reparation, and what each reparation is for. Sr. Lucia provided this information for us in a letter dated June 12, 1930. In it she tells us that Our Lord appeared to her in the convent chapel on the night of May 29-30, 1930, and revealed to her the meaning of the five Saturdays. Sr. Lucia quotes Our Lord's words to her:

> "Daughter, the motive is simple: there are five ways in which people offend and blaspheme against the Immaculate Heart of Mary: there are blasphemies (1) against her Immaculate Conception, (2) against her Virginity, (3) against her Divine Maternity, refusing at the same time to accept her as the Mother of all mankind, (4) by those who try publicly to implant in the hearts of children indifference, contempt and even hate against this Immaculate Mother, and (5) by those who insult her directly in her sacred images."

It is obvious from all of the above how important this devotion really is. In the following chapters, I will reflect on each of the five reasons why Our Lord wants this reparation paid to the Immaculate Heart of His Blessed Mother and ours, too!

CHAPTER 2

The First Reparation of the Five First Saturdays: For Those Who Blaspheme Against the Immaculate Conception

"I am the Immaculate Conception!" That is the way the Blessed Virgin Mary identified herself at Lourdes to St. Bernadette when the saint had asked who she was. What a marvelous description, one that brings great joy to all who love Our Lady. She is, as a Protestant writer once put it, "our tainted human nature's solitary boast!"

The Immaculate Conception of the Blessed Virgin Mary is especially dear to devout Catholics. It expresses the belief of the Church that Our Lady, through a singular grace and privilege of Almighty God, and through the foreseen merits of Jesus Christ, the Savior of the human race, and in view of her becoming the Mother of God, was preserved free from Original Sin and given a fullness of grace from the first moment of her conception. This was defined as a revealed dogma of the Catholic Faith by Blessed Pope Pius IX in his decree, *Ineffabilis Deus* on December 8, 1854.

This privilege of Our Lady is one of the most cherished of Catholic beliefs. It is also one of the most important. It shows Jesus' complete power and victory over sin. Jesus came to save us from our sins. Did He not say, *"The Son of Man has come to search out and save what was lost"* (Luke 19:10)? He does this in various ways. In Baptism, He takes away the guilt of Original Sin (and of any personal sins that someone over the age of reason may have committed), while at the same time infusing into that soul a share in His own divine life that He merited for us by His redemptive death. In the Sacrament of Penance, Jesus takes away our personal sins committed after Baptism through the power to forgive sins, which He gave to His Apostles on Easter night (cf. *n* 20:22-23), and which has been passed down over the centuries to His bishops and priests.

Now in both these cases, sin has already affected the person, leaving traces of wounds and weaknesses in its wake, even after they have been forgiven! In the case of Our Lady, her privilege was so great that Original Sin (and consequently personal sin as well) never touched her soul. Our Lady would have incurred the guilt of Original Sin because St. Paul says that all men sinned in Adam (cf. Romans 5:12).

8

But in her case, her privilege was an extraordinary form of Redemption. Our Lady was redeemed by being preserved from Original Sin in view of the foreseen merits of Jesus, her Divine Son rather than being delivered from Original Sin after she had suffered from it. Let us use a comparison by way of example. It would be one thing for a doctor to use his medical skill to heal a patient after an accident. (In a sense, this is what Jesus did for all the baptized!) It would be quite another thing for the doctor to prevent the patient from having an accident in the first place. (This is like what Jesus did for His Mother!) At the same time, she was filled with such an extraordinary fullness of Sanctifying Grace that some saints believed it surpassed the combined holiness of all the angels and saints together!

WHY IS THE "IMMACULATE CONCEPTION" BLASPHEMED?

It Foreshadows Jesus' Complete Victory Over Sin

This blasphemy, no doubt, comes ultimately from Satan himself. The Devil inspires it for many reasons. First, he is angry at Jesus' power and victory which this dogma represents. He knows that at the end of time, any power God allows him to tempt us with will cease completely. He foresees this conquest of Christ over him and his legions, in Our Lady's complete victory of sinlessness all through her life from the first moment of her conception. He deeply resents Our Lady's immaculate holiness. It meant that he did not have, even for one instant, any power or influence over her. Our Lady was like a bright light shining through the darkness of Satan's control and deceit. Satan was helpless to block that light, to stop it, to prevent it from showing the evil he intended to inflict on all mankind. Therefore, he inspires anyone, whether they be among his conscious followers in the occult or simply people who are very weak morally, to express hate, ridicule and contempt against Our Lady's marvelous privilege.

It Reveals Our Lady as the "Woman"
who crushes the Head of Satan

Another reason the devil hates the privilege of Our Lady's Immaculate Conception is because he sees the Virgin Mary in a special way under this title as the "Woman" who will crush his head! Immediately after Satan deceived our first parents into committing the Original Sin, God said to him, *"I will put enmity between you and the Woman, and between your offspring and hers; she will crush your head, while you strike at her heel!"* (Genesis 3:15, Vulgate translation) When God spoke of the "Woman," He was obviously not referring to Eve of old to crush Satan's head, since she had just personally sinned by pride (wanting to be as a god) and disobedience (eating the forbidden fruit) at his deception.

Who then is the "Woman?" The Church sees this as a reference to Mary, the Mother of Jesus and our Mother, too! Jesus Himself twice refers to His own Mother as "Woman." (When I was studying Sacred

Scripture in the seminary, they taught us that Jesus' reference to His own Mother as "Woman" was an absolutely unique usage among all ancient Hebrew and Greek literature.) The first usage occurs at the wedding feast of Cana (cf. John 2:1-11), when Jesus says to His Mother, *"Woman, how does this concern of yours involve me? My hour has not yet come."* Moved by the confident trust of His Mother, Jesus then works His first miracle by changing water into wine, thus also inspiring His disciples to believe in Him. The second usage occurs at the cross on Calvary (cf. John 19:25-27) when Jesus gives His Mother the care of all His followers represented by John, the "beloved disciple," saying to her, *"Woman, behold your son!"*

God's words to Satan in Genesis 3:15 are often cited as a "proof text" to support the fact that the dogma of the Immaculate Conception was revealed by God in Sacred Scripture. How is this so? The words we want to focus on are: *"I will put enmity between you* (meaning, the serpent, Satan) *and the Woman"* (meaning, Our Lady, the New Eve). The key word here is "enmity." Enmity means a very bitter hatred. Now, despite how strong our English word enmity is, it cannot convey the full force and intense meaning of the original Hebrew word. The Hebrew root of this word implied such a bitter mutual repulsion between the two, that not for even the briefest moment could they tolerate being in each other's presence. Therefore, Our Lady and Satan would not want to be near each other! So how could

11

Satan have had an influence over the soul of Our Lady, even for one moment? And without such influence or control, the Immaculate Conception represented the beginning of the destruction of Satan's universal influence over sinful mankind. It was, to use God's words, the beginning of the crushing of his head!

It Prepared Our Lady for Her Divine Maternity

The Immaculate Conception was a marvelous gift from Our Heavenly Father to the Virgin Mary in view of preparing her to become the Mother of His own Divine Son. This privilege separated Our Lady from any direct personal contact with sin. She was as a result sinless and grace-filled! At the moment the Incarnation occurred during the Annunciation, Jesus took His very Flesh and Blood from the absolutely pure body united to the immaculate soul of the Blessed Virgin Mary! This sinlessness is reflected in the Archangel Gabriel's salutation to Our Lady at the Annunciation: *"Hail, full of grace, the Lord is with you. Blessed are you among women!"* (Luke 1:28) In view of this wondrous event, Satan's fury no doubt knew no limits (cf. Revelation 12:12). This is an added reason why he has been relentless in stirring up blasphemy and contempt among his followers against this special privilege of Our Lady!

REPARATION FOR THESE BLASPEMIES IS IMPORTANT

Reparation in this instance is directed at restoring

the honor due to Our Lady for God's great privilege to her in view of her becoming the Mother of God. Blasphemy has seriously offended God by dishonoring the extraordinary grace He gave her in her Immaculate Conception. Our reparation atones for this grave dishonor, while praising and venerating the Virgin Mary with appropriate devotion. Did not Our Lady herself, while carrying Jesus physically in her womb, say in her Magnificat: *"God who is mighty has done great things for me, and holy is His name"*? (Luke 1:49)

Besides offering the first of the Five Saturdays' devotion in reparation for the blasphemies against the Immaculate Conception, a person may also choose to wear the Miraculous Medal that was entrusted by Our Lady to St. Catherine Labouré. Since its design was revealed to the saint in a vision, we must truly say it was formed in heaven. It bore the significant prayer to Our Lady, "O Mary conceived without sin, pray for us who have recourse to Thee!" Besides wearing the Miraculous Medal, we should repeat that prayer often, thus making added reparation for blasphemies against the Immaculate Conception. Finally, we should encourage others to practice the Five Saturdays' devotion, and to honor the privilege of Our Lady's Immaculate Conception, thus making further reparation for the blasphemies she has endured. All of this will obtain the special powerful protection of Our Lady against sin and Satan's power in our lives.

CHAPTER 3
The Second Reparation
of the Five First Saturdays

For Those Who Blaspheme Against the Perpetual Virginity of Mary

One of the most popular titles of Our Blessed Lady is to call her the "Virgin Mary!" This is very fitting because it is rooted in Sacred Scripture. When St. Luke described the Annunciation event, he twice referred to Our Lady as "virgin." *"In the sixth month, the angel Gabriel was sent from God to a town of Galilee named Nazareth, to a virgin betrothed to a man named Joseph, of the house of David. The virgin's name was Mary"* (Luke 1:26-27).

St. Matthew, in his Gospel account, also stresses Our Lady's virginity, emphasizing that the conception of Jesus occurred without Our Lady having marital relations with St. Joseph. *"Now this is how the birth of Jesus Christ came about. When His mother Mary* was engaged to Joseph, but before they lived together, she was found with child through the power of the Holy Spirit. Joseph, her husband, an upright man, unwilling to expose her to the law, decided to divorce her quietly. Such was his intention when suddenly the angel of the Lord appeared in a dream and said to him: 'Joseph, son of David, have no fear about taking Mary as your wife. It is by the Holy Spirit that she has conceived this child. She is to have a son and you are to name Him Jesus because He will save His people from their sins.' All this happened to fulfill what the Lord had said through the prophet: 'The virgin shall be with child and give birth to a son, and they shall call him Emmanuel' (Isaiah 7:14), a name which means 'God is with us.' When Joseph awoke, he did as the angel of the Lord had directed him and received her into his home. He had no relations with her at any time before she bore a son, whom He named Jesus" (Matthew 1:10-25).

Our Lady's Virginity was Perpetual

These two Gospel passages clearly state that Our Lady was truly a virgin at the moment she conceived Christ within her womb by the power of the Holy Spirit. In fact, Our Lady's virginity was to be perpetual. This is a dogma of the Catholic Church. St. Clement of Alexandria (d. 215 AD) was one of the earliest Fathers of the Church to express this fact: "O great mystery! Mary, an incorrupt virgin conceived, after conception brought forth as a virgin, after childbirth she remained a virgin." The First

Lateran Council (647 AD), under Pope St. Martin I, later defined Our Lady's perpetual virginity when it condemned anyone who did not acknowledge with the Fathers of the Church that "the holy and ever virgin and immaculate Mary was really and truly the Mother of God. Inasmuch as she, in the fullness of time, and without seed, conceived by the Holy Spirit, God the Word Himself, Who before all time was born of God the Father, and without loss of integrity brought Him forth, and after His birth preserved her virginity inviolate."

This dogma was traditionally expressed in the formula that Mary was virgin "before, during and after the birth" of Jesus. We have already seen how the meaning of the phrase, "before the birth" of Jesus is clear from the Gospel accounts above. Let us look briefly at the other two phrases. "During the birth" of Jesus grew out of the understanding of the Church, enlightened by the Holy Spirit. It expresses the belief that at the moment of her giving birth to Jesus, through a special divine action, Mary did not lose the physical signs of her virginity. The Fathers of the Church would say that the womb of the Blessed Mother remained closed and intact, and that Jesus passed through the enclosure of her womb much as He passed through the walls of the room where the Apostles were gathered on Easter night with the doors bolted closed (cf. John 20:19). Furthermore, Mary's giving birth to Jesus was painless, as is reflected in the fact that Our Lady herself *wrapped [Jesus] in swaddling clothes and laid Him in a manger*" (cf. Luke 2:7), something which would have been nearly impossible for a woman who had just suffered the excruciating pains of childbirth! If Our Lady did not have a painless virgin birth, St. Joseph would more likely have done these things!

"After the birth" of Jesus requires a somewhat longer explanation because certain objections have been raised against it over the centuries. This phrase refers to the dogmatic belief in Catholic tradition that Our Lady never had marital relations with St. Joseph even after the birth of Jesus, but preserved her virginity intact for the rest of her life. Our Lady, as we shall see, was quite concerned to preserve her virginity before conceiving Jesus, so why should we assume she would surrender her virginity afterwards?

Let us look very briefly at the source of the major objections we find here. The biggest difficulty, raised from early Christian centuries, is that Sacred Scripture speaks of Jesus' "brothers" (cf. Matthew 13:55: Mark 3:31-35; Mark 6:3). How could Our Lady have remained a perpetual virgin if she had other sons after the birth of Jesus? One explanation given by St. Epiphanius (d. 403 AD) was that the "brothers of the Lord" were really sons of St. Joseph by a prior marriage, but there is no evidence at all in the Gospels to support this idea. Another and better explanation is the fact that neither Hebrew nor Aramaic, Our Lord's spoken language, had a specific word for "*cousin.*" The word "*brother*" was commonly used to indicate actual cousins. (Even today the word "*brother*" is used broadly in certain ethnic groups to include simple companions, or in my own case as a Franciscan friar to include my fellow religious. Now in neither case is there any blood relationship, but simply a fraternal bond.) Furthermore, these "brothers of the Lord" are never called the children of Mary, and in fact, two of them, James and Joseph (cf. Matthew 13:55; called James and Joses in Mark 6:3), are explicitly said to be the children of another Mary who is certainly not Our Lady (cf. Matthew 27:56). A final observation is that elsewhere in the New Testament, the word *"brother"* is used in a general way to indicate a fellow disciple, not a relative (cf. Acts 1:15; 1 Corinthians 5:11, 15:6).

Our Lady's Intention
Was to Remain a Virgin Always

Our Lady's intention to remain a virgin can be seen in her response to the angel Gabriel's message that she was to become a mother: *"How can this be since I do not know man?"* (Luke 1:34). Catholic tradition, going all the way back to the early Fathers of the Church, has always understood Our Lady's question to imply that she had already been inspired by the Holy Spirit to consecrate her virginity to God. If this was not the case, and she was intending to have marital relations with St. Joseph after they lived together as husband and wife, then it logically follows that she would have assumed this was how she would conceive, as the angel had foretold. Thus, her question would make no sense. Therefore, Our Lady's question can only be logically interpreted to mean: *"Not only have I not had marital relations with St. Joseph during this time of our solemn engagement, but even after our marriage I will not have marital relations with him!"* We may then conclude that Our Lady is here not only stating the fact that she is a virgin at that moment, but also that she is determined to remain a virgin always!

The Meaning and Importance of
Our Lady's Perpetual Virginity

Consecrated virginity, or virginity as a permanent state, was unknown in the Old Testament. It was an aspect of that *"celibacy for the sake of the Kingdom of Heaven"* (cf. Matthew 19:10-12) which Jesus taught for those who were willing to accept it in the New Testament. Our Lady was, no doubt, inspired to her perpetual virginity by the light of the Holy Spirit. Her sinlessness and overwhelming holiness allowed her such openness to the inspirations of the Holy Spirit, that she not only recognized virginity consecrated to God as a spiritual treasure, but she steadfastly consecrated her own virginity to God. St. Therese of Lisieux, our newest Doctor of the Church, was of the opinion that if Our Lady could only become the Mother of Jesus by breaking her vow of virginity to God, she would not have become Jesus' Mother. The Little Flower was convinced that Our Lady would never take back what she had already given to God.

Church historians point out that the doctrine of Mary's perpetual virginity was to become an ideal for many Christian men and women who wanted to give their lives more fully to Christ. Thus, the ideal of consecrated celibacy in both the priesthood and religious life found support in the model of the Virgin Mary! Unfortunately, after Vatican Council II, some liberal Catholic theologians, in an air of theological ferment within the Church at the time, began to reinvestigate long accepted truths with an attitude of complete freedom, as if they were not defined Church teachings. Thus, the perpetual virginity of Our Lady, accepted as dogma for over fifteen centuries since the first Lateran Council (AD 649), began to be questioned and rejected by some within the Church!. Could it not be that, in the social climate of the late 1960s and the 1970s, when Western culture was experiencing the devastating effects of the so-called "Sexual Revolution" and some Catholics were promoting a "new sexual morality" that was nothing but a distortion of authentic Catholic moral teaching, that certain people rejected the teaching and example of Our Lady's perpetual virginity, because it was a moral rebuke to the sexual license they were spreading? As Archbishop Fulton J. Sheen put it, "No one becomes a heretic for the way they want to think, but for the way they want to live!"

The late Archbishop, a great devotee of Our Lady, also used to say: "Where devotion to the Blessed Virgin Mary is strong, womanhood, motherhood and purity are all held in great respect!" Devotion to the Virgin Mary is a strong bulwark against the sins of the flesh! If it is rejected, the road to sexual promiscuity would open even wider.

Consecrated or perpetual virginity embraced publicly or privately, is an outstanding sign of the virtue of purity. This is why the sex-crazed society we live in not only rejects it, but attacks it viciously. This author remembers hearing slogans during the turbulent 60s and 70s like "Down with virginity." In the same way, we hear constant demands, both from inside and outside the Church that priestly celibacy should be done away with. Since the perpetual virginity of Our Lady is a model and encouragement for consecrated celibacy, it is no wonder it that has been the object of much blasphemy, which we counter by our First Saturday reparation.

Virginity, seen as the chastity lived by young people before marriage, is another important expression of this virtue. Today, many teenagers are ridiculed by their peers if they admit they are still "virgins." It has become a widespread assumption that every teenager is "sexually active." Thank God and Our Lady, that that is not so. Many young people recognize that their gift of sexuality is meant to be a special gift reserved for married life. They struggle hard to maintain their virginity before marriage. Today, we must encourage young people to look to the Virgin Mary as their example, and to seek her protection with their prayers. There are also a few clever little reminders that help, too! One is a "chastity ring," worn to remind young people to say, "I don't" before they say, "I do!" Another is a chastity button that says, "I'm worth waiting for!"

The Virgin Mary is a great support to all of us in our practice of purity according to our state in life. No wonder the world blasphemes her perpetual virginity! Let us make reparation for these blasphemies. In this way we will win through the intercession of the Immaculate Heart of Mary, greater graces for purity for the virtuous to remain faithful, and for those whose lives have been caught up in sexual chaos to return to the Divine Mercy of Jesus!

For Those Who Blaspheme Against Mary's Divine Motherhood

Belief in Mary as the Mother of God is one of the most cherished beliefs of Catholics. This privilege of Our Lady is the basis and reason for all the other privileges she received from God. It was precisely because she was chosen from all women to be the Mother of Jesus Christ, the Son of God Who took His human nature from her, that she was conceived without Original Sin (the privilege of her Immaculate Conception), that she remained a virgin before, during and after the birth of Jesus (the privilege of her Perpetual Virginity), that she played a very special part with Jesus in His mission of redeeming the world (her privilege as Co-Redemptrix), and that she was assumed body and soul into Heaven when her earthly life was ended (the privilege of her Assumption).

It was only fitting that Our Lady enjoyed all of these privileges in order to fulfill her exalted vocation from God! After all, if we could have chosen our own earthly mother and then be allowed to give her the choicest blessings to make her the best of mothers, would we not have done so?

Then how much more would Jesus do that, since He in fact did choose His own Mother, and then endowed her with all those gifts that would make her the very best of all mothers!

It would be very important to clarify at this point exactly what we mean, as well as what we do not mean, when we call Mary "the Mother of God." Let us start with what we do not mean. When we call Our Lady "the Mother of God," we do not mean she gave birth to Jesus in His Divinity. Many people, especially among our separated brethren, are often under this grave misunderstanding!

As God, the Second Divine Person existed from all eternity. That means He had no beginning, and He will never have an ending! If Mary gave birth to Jesus in His Divinity, then that would mean that Jesus is not God, since God could not have a beginning. It would also make Our Lady appear that she was some sort of "super-goddess" which she is absolutely not!

Mothers are always Mothers of Persons

What then, do we mean when we call Mary "the Mother of God"? To try to explain this simply but clearly, we must use two words taken from Philosophy. They are "nature" and "person." Nature describes the makeup of something, with all its powers and abilities. Nature answers the question, "What is it?" For example, it can be an angel, a man or woman, an animal or even God. Each of them have the powers and abilities that are part of their nature.

God, by His Divine Nature, has infinite knowledge and power, and can create things out of nothing. No other nature, because it is created and limited, has the powers of God's Nature! An angel, by his angelic nature, which is totally spiritual, has vast infused knowledge and power, and can do many things human beings cannot.

Men and women, by their human nature, which is partly spiritual (their soul) and partly material (their body), have the ability to reason with their intellect and to freely choose with their wills, as well as the abilities that come from their bodily powers, such as the use of the senses, movement, and reproduction. An animal - whose nature is purely material - has the ability to use senses, move about and reproduce its species, but it lacks the human being's ability to reason intellectually and to choose freely. Animals are governed largely by instinct.

"Person" refers to any being having intelligence and free will, and who is responsible for his or her actions and the consequences of them. We refer to the "person" as the "agent" or the one who acts through the powers of her or her nature. Person answers the question, "Who is it?" It follows, then, that there are only three categories of "persons;" a Divine Person, such as God the Father; an angelic person, such as St. Michael, and a human person, such as St. Therese. Animals, because they lack the ability to reason intellectually and to choose freely, are not "persons" in this philosophical sense.

Let us apply these ideas of "nature" and "person" to Jesus, and therefore to why we call Mary, His Mother, "the Mother of God." What the Catholic Church teaches as her defined dogma is that in Jesus, there are two natures (one Divine and the other human), but only one Person (the Second Divine Person of the Blessed Trinity). From all eternity, without beginning and without end, Jesus was the Second Divine Person, with His Divine Nature, which He possessed with God the Father and God the Holy Spirit. He had the same infinite powers to create, to redeem and to sanctify as they did.

What happened in the moment of the Incarnation was that this Second Person, while keeping His Divine Nature, also took a human nature. He did this by taking His flesh and blood from the womb of the Virgin Mary, when the power of the Holy Spirit came upon her to accomplish this greatest event in human history. As we profess in the Apostles' Creed: "He (Jesus) was conceived by the Holy Spirit, born of the Virgin Mary…" Though Jesus has a human consciousness, a human intelligence and a human free will, He is not a human person. Rather, the Second Divine Person now acts through the human nature

He acquired from Our Lady. In other words, the "agent" responsible for acting through the human nature of Jesus is a Divine Person.

Now, let us apply all this to Our Lady's title of "Mother of God." A human mother is always the mother of a person. Although the mother and father together conceived the child, and God alone infused the soul into the child at the moment of conception (which is why we respect all human life from the moment of conception), the mother is called the mother of the whole person. For example, we say: "This is John's mother" or "This is Anne's mother." We do not say: This is the mother of John's body" or "This is the mother of Anne's body." Motherhood always applies to a person. And the only person in Jesus Christ, Who is fully God and fully man, is the second Divine Person. Therefore, since Mary is the mother of Jesus' human nature, we can say of her: "Mary is the Mother of Jesus;" "Mary is the Mother of One Who is a Divine Person;" "Mary is the Mother of God."

The Important Teaching
of the Council of Ephesus

This teaching of the Catholic Church was declared in a special way at the Ecumenical Council of Ephesus in 431 AD. (Ephesus is located in modern Turkey. A strong Catholic tradition says that St. John the Beloved Disciple, who received Our Lady into his care at the foot the cross, later in a time of persecution took her to Ephesus where there was a large Christian

29

community. It was there that Our Lady died, and she was assumed into Heaven. It is still a site of Christian pilgrimage.) At the time, some Christians had asked Nestorius, then Patriarch of Constantinople, if Mary could be called in Greek, *"Theotokos,"* which meant literally the "God-bearer" or "Mother of God." The Patriarch answered that Mary could not be called *"Theotokos,"* but only *"Christotokos,"* "the bearer of Christ" implying that in Jesus there was a human person (Christ) as well as a Divine Person (the Second Divine Person). This teaching became the heresy we call *"Nestorianism"* after its founder. It undermined the whole reality of the Incarnation. What it implied was that God did not really become man, but He simply entered into union with a human person and coexisted there. Thus, according to this heresy, in Jesus of Nazareth, there would have been a Divine Person with a Divine Nature as well as a human person with a human nature. Furthermore, since the "agent" working in the human nature of Jesus would be only a human person, his actions would have had only limited merit. Only a Divine Person can perform an action of infinite merit.

So, if only a human (Christ) died on the cross, the merit of his death would not have been sufficient to redeem the world! That would mean that all of us would still be in our sins, because a purely human person could not atone for our sins.

However, when we maintain the true Catholic teaching that the only Person in Jesus was a Divine Person, then His dying on the cross would be meritorious to redeem the whole world! The Council of Ephesus, led by St. Cyril of Alexandria, condemned the heretical teaching of Nestorious and proclaimed Our Lady as "Theotokos," "the God-bearer" or "the Mother of God." The Christians of Ephesus were so overjoyed that they held a night-long procession throughout the streets of Ephesus chanting, "Theotokos! Theotokos!" It is our same joy to proclaim Mary as the "Mother of God!"

It is the intention for the third of the First Five Saturdays of the month to make reparation for those who, whether from misunderstanding or from deliberate disbelief, deny, or ridicule, or blaspheme this very special Catholic teaching about Our Blessed Mother! As she herself, inspired by the Holy Spirit, proclaimed in her great song of thanksgiving, her "Magnificat:"

> *"From this day all generations will call me blessed; the Almighty has done great things for me, and holy is His Name!"*

CHAPTER 5
The Third Reparation
of the Five First Saturdays
(Part Two)

For Those Who Blaspheme
Mary's Spiritual Motherhood
of All God's People

Archbishop Fulton J. Sheen often said that Our Lady has a two-fold motherhood. The first was her physical motherhood. Being the Mother of Jesus, the Eternal Word made flesh, she is truly the Mother of God, and this is her "Divine Maternity." This motherhood was fulfilled when, having conceived by the power of the Holy Spirit at the Annunciation, she gave birth to Jesus at Bethlehem on that first beautiful day we call Christmas. As her conceiving of Jesus was a virginal conception, so her giving birth to Him in the stable at Bethlehem was also a virginal birth. She neither lost her physical integrity, nor did she suffer any pangs of childbirth. The Fathers of the Church offered this explanation of the virgin-birth of Jesus: He miraculously passed through the wall of Our Lady's womb much as He passed through the walls of the Upper Room in Jerusalem when He appeared to the Apostles after His Resurrection (cf. John 20:26). This is because there was no sin involved in either mother or Child. She was the Immaculate Conception; He was innocence itself. Remember that the pangs of childbirth were the result of Original Sin (cf. Genesis 3:16) and Our Lady was spared both the guilt of that sin and its punishment!

Our Lady's second motherhood was spiritual. This is her motherhood of all the brothers and sisters of Jesus, making them also her own true sons and daughters. Since this motherhood is an important part of God's plan of salvation for all mankind, we may appropriately refer to it as Our Lady's "Redemptive Maternity." It actually follows from her "Divine Maternity," and is inseparably connected with it! Why? As St. Louis-Marie de Monfort put it, a mother cannot give birth to a head without also giving birth to its body, composed of its many bodily members. Therefore, by her "Divine Maternity," Our Lady gave physical life to Jesus, the Head of the Mystical Body, the Church. By her "Redemptive Maternity," Our Lady assisted in giving new supernatural life to all the faithful, all the members of Jesus' Mystical Body, the Church. In the first birth,

Mary gives life to Jesus in the flesh: *"the Word became flesh and made His dwelling among us"* (John 1:14). In the second birth, Mary cooperates in giving new life in the Spirit to those who are *"begotten of water and the Spirit"* (John 3:5).

Mary's "Redemptive Maternity" Differs From Her "Divine Maternity"

The contrast of Mary's second motherhood with the first is very striking. Her "redemptive Maternity" takes place on Calvary. There was actually a new birth taking place there at the very moment of Jesus' death. When the Roman centurion pierced the heart of Jesus with his lance, we read that *"immediately blood and water flowed out"* (John 19:34). The Fathers of the Church said that the blood here represented the Holy Eucharist, while the water represented Baptism. These are the two main Sacraments of the Church, since Baptism is our birth to new life in Christ while the Holy Eucharist is the Bread of life! Together the blood and water represent the new life in Christ that we have received. It is actually Jesus Himself who is being formed in us or, in a sense, coming to birth in us. Because of this, we can say with St. Paul: *"The life I live now is not my own; Christ is living in me. I still live my human life, but it is a life of faith in the Son of God, Who loved me and gave Himself for me"* (Galatians 2:20). Our new life in the Spirit focuses on Jesus coming to live spiritually within us. So, if Jesus is being born again spiritually within us, Our Lady needs to be there!

Another contrast in Mary's second motherhood was that while her giving birth to Jesus at Bethlehem was painless because there was no sin in either Child or mother, there was great pain on Calvary. Though Our Lady was absolutely sinless and *"filled with grace"* (cf. Luke 1:28), her "new children" were steeped in sin! Because of their sins, they were in danger of being lost forever in Hell. That is why Jesus, with an infinite love, offered Himself in obedience to the Heavenly Father's Will, as a substituted "Victim," *"obediently accepting death, even death on a cross"* (Philippians 2:8) to suffer in reparation for our sins. Her pain then was the sorrow within her pierced motherly heart not only to witness the death of her Jesus hanging in such unspeakable pain upon the cross, but also to unite with Him in His Self-offering to the Father. Our Lady literally had to will, in accordance with the Heavenly Father's plan, the suffering and death of her "first-born Son" so that a multitude of spiritual sons and daughters might come to new life in union with Jesus.

Our Lord confirmed His mother's "Redemptive Maternity" by His own words from the cross: *"Near the cross of Jesus there stood His mother, His mother's sister, Mary the wife of Clopas, and Mary Magdalene. Seeing His mother there with the disciple whom He loved, Jesus said to His mother, 'Woman, there is your son!' In turn He said to the disciple, 'There is your mother!'* (John 19:25-27). St. Bernard of Clairvaux captures the magnitude of Our Lady's maternal love and suffering at that moment when he writes: "Truly, O Blessed Mother...were those words: 'Woman, behold your son,' not more than a sword to you, truly piercing your heart, cutting through to the division between soul and spirit? What an exchange! John is given to you in the place of Jesus, the servant in place of the Lord, the disciple in place of the Master; the son of Zebedee replaces the Son of God, a mere man replaces God Himself! How could these words not pierce your most loving heart, when the mere remembrance of them breaks ours, hearts of stone and iron though they are!"

Our Lady's "Redemptive Maternity" Lasts Until the End of the World

Our Lady can never forget her redemptive maternal mission which will continue in the world until the end of time. It is most precious to Our Lady because it was given to her by her Divine Son in the midst of His sufferings and hers! Furthermore, because it involves redemption from our sinfulness, it will never be free of suffering. Well might St. Paul's words regarding his converts apply to Our Lady's relationship to us, her spiritual children: *"You are my children, and you put me back in labor pains until Christ is formed in you!"* (Galatians 4:19) This is why, in connection with Fatima, we speak of Our Lady's "Immaculate and Sorrowful Heart."

This redemptive motherhood is very dear to Our Lady. Her maternal love for us knows no bounds! This is why it offends the honor of Our Lady when people deny her redemptive motherhood or, worse still, ridicule and blaspheme it. Why would anyone do these things? Perhaps our answer can be found in a traditional principle of the spiritual life, "Grace builds on nature." It means, among other things, that many spiritual or religious problems actually have their basis in our human relationships. In other words, many have difficulty accepting Mary's spiritual motherhood because they have significant difficulties relating to their own human mothers. We will look at some of these relationships so as to identify the underlying cause of the problem, and then try to offer some remedies that can free the person to be open to Our Lady's motherhood.

Some Possible Reason
for this Blasphemy

Some people experienced a lack of love and affection from their mothers. For example, a situation where a mother never tells her own child that she loves him or her, and yet the child deeply craves being told that! Or a situation where a mother never showed any external signs of affection, such as a kiss or a hug. Such people often experience this lacking as a rejection, as a sense that "I am not good enough!" Because of this hurt and the insecurity it breeds, they may be afraid of reaching out to Our Lady as their mother for fear she may also reject them!

What these people must try to do is to separate their earthly mother from their Heavenly mother. They must recognize the pain of what they did not receive growing up, and try with heal these scars by working

38

at bettering their relationship to their mothers, if this is possible. But they must clearly separate such negative experiences from Our Lady, toward whom they should attempt to reach out trustingly.

Another source of difficulty can be the situation where one's mother played "favorites," thus while obviously loving a brother or a sister, she neglected this one child. This can leave the impression that one must always compete to win the attention and love of a mother, even Our Blessed Mother. To counter this insecurity, the person must be told that Our Lady's love for one of her children does not take away from the love of any of her other children. She loves each of us as if we were her only children on earth! Padre Pio said he experienced Our Lady's motherly love and care in precisely this manner!

A third difficulty would be for people who experienced their mother's love as "manipulative" or "controlling." Mother showed her love clearly when the child was well behaved or did well in school. If not, she withheld her love and affection for very prolonged periods. This can breed in the child the feeling that all love is "conditional," and if I do not meet the conditions, I will not be loved. It also makes love appear as "uncertain," because I will never know when that love will be withheld. To overcome such insecurity, the person must recognize that Our Lady's love is never "hot or cold," or unpredictable. Even when Jesus and Mary withdraw all emotional feelings from their love (this is "spiritual dryness"), they do so only to help us mature in faith, and not to put us on an emotional roller coaster!

A further difficulty can come when a mother has been abusive, whether verbally, physically or even sexually. This requires a great deal of healing, and may, for a considerable time, prevent one's relationship to Our Blessed Mother from developing as it should. Much prayer is needed to forgive such past hurts and allow reconciliation, if possible, with one's mother. As healing on the natural level grows, there will be greater openness to Our Lady on the supernatural level.

A final area of difficulty stems from various "prejudices." In some cultures, for example, women are looked upon as "second-class" citizens. Their importance and dignity as creatures of God are denied. Such people would most likely have difficulty accepting another woman as "mother." The same applies to many people in our present culture of sexual license and perversion, who lack a healthy orientation toward women. They may well find the childlike trust and confidence involved in accepting Mary as our spiritual mother altogether too much! Those who reject motherhood in general because of a pro-abortion attitude will also likely reject Our Lady's motherhood. Finally, some non-Catholic Christians may reject Our Lady's spiritual maternity because it sounds "too Catholic." Since Marian devotion is strongly linked with Catholic piety, it might require an admission of a truth they might not want to concede. They need to look objectively at Mary's motherhood, and not make it a bone of contention.

When we offer our Five First Saturday a devotion to Our Lady, let us pray and sacrifice for all these and many others who experience obstacles to their acceptance of Our Lady's spiritual motherhood in their lives! Our Lady loves them all, and is simply waiting to extend her maternal love and care even to those of her children who out of ignorance, fear, or prejudice reject the motherhood she obtained at so great a price. To quote St. Bernard's sermon once more: "If Jesus could die in body, could Mary not die with Him in spirit? He died in body through a love greater than anyone had ever known! She died in spirit through a love unlike any other since His!"

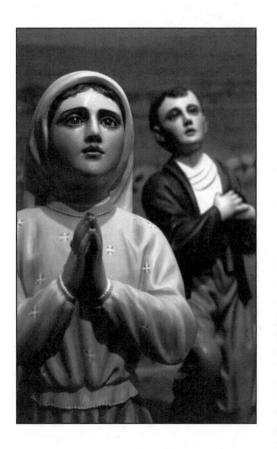

CHAPTER 6
The Fourth Reparation
of the Five First Saturdays

For Those Who Alienate Children From Devotion to Our Lady

The Gospel records the story of a group of mothers who were approaching Jesus with their little children in order for Him to place His hands on them and bless them. The Apostles mistakenly thought that the children were at best a distraction to Our Lord, and at worst an annoyance He did not want or need.

So the Apostles were stopping the mothers and children from approaching Jesus, turning them away. Our Lord's response was quick and clear:

> "Let the children come to Me. Do not hinder them. The kingdom of God belongs to such as these.' And He laid His hand on their heads..."

43

(Matthew 19:14-15)
Begin Speaking about Mary
While the Children are Still Young

It is clear from this incident how much Our Lord wants children to come to Him! From their earliest years, the young must be taught about Jesus, about His life, death and resurrection, about His Church, emphasizing her doctrine and Sacraments. This includes in a very special way the Church's rich treasure of teaching and devotion to the Blessed Virgin Mary. She is Jesus' mother, and must therefore be loved, honored and respected along with Him! She is also our mother, given to us by Jesus Himself from the cross of Calvary: *"Woman, behold your son!...Behold your mother!"* (John 19:26-27) And is there anything more instinctive than for a little child to seek his or her mother?

Even from a child's earliest years, he or she can begin to grasp a love for Our Lady in keeping with his or her stage of development. Please allow me to illustrate with two examples drawn from my own family's experience. One involves a niece of mine and the other a nephew. This particular niece would often visit one of her uncles, who had a statue of Our Lady in his backyard. We members of the family would often observe her standing for long periods of time in front of the statue, seemingly engrossed in an animated conversation with the Blessed Mother! One can only imagine what passed between the Immaculate Heart of Our Lady and the innocent heart of a child! The story of my nephew involves a child who was only two years old at the time, or as my brother often put it, in "the terrible twos"! When my brother would bring his little son to Mass on Sundays, he told me that sometimes he was very well behaved, but other times he got quite restless. Well, on one of those occasions when the little guy was restless, my brother walked with him out into the foyer of the church where there was a statue of Our Lady of Grace with her arms reaching outward. As soon as my little nephew saw the statue, he announced to his father, "I'm going to give Mary five!" He promptly went over and gave Our Lady "the high five sign" which he loved to give me (and I suspect others, too!) when I visited! It was my nephew's innocent way, even at the age of two, of showing Our Lady his love for her and that she was special to him! Now, I am not suggesting that we all give Our Lady "the high five sign," but it does represent how easily a child can be taught to honor and revere the Mother of God and our Mother, too!

Silence about Our Lady will have
Disastrous Effects for a Child

The foundation of Marian devotion should ordinarily be given in the home. Word and example must go together to assure that it will have a lasting effect. When children hear and see that Our Lady is important to their parents, she becomes important to them also. Many parents today, wanting to adopt what they mistakenly believe is certain "broadmindedness" about religious truths, take the attitude that they will not teach their children anything specific about religion. They say, "I will let my children grow up, and then they can make up their own minds about what they want to believe or not!" (You will notice that they do not allow these same children to make up their own minds about whether they want to go the school or not!)

For a child to wait until he or she grows up to learn basic truths such as those of religion will be too late! The fallacy in this thinking is that to say nothing, is in effect to say something. The human mind at birth is what philosophers would call a "tabula rasa," that is, "a blank sheet." To have any knowledge in the mind, it must come either through experience or by teaching. Therefore, to say nothing about religious truths, - in this case Our Blessed Mother – is to deprive the child of even knowing she exists. After all, you can only come to know the existence of other people when you have been introduced to them, whether by teaching about them, such as when we study about people from history, or by a personal encounter with that individual. Silence on the part of parents, then, conveys to the child either that Our Lady does not exist, or that she is not very important! At the same time, silence on such important religious truths leaves a kind of intellectual vacuum which will very likely sooner or later be filled with erroneous ideas and false moral values. These may come from distorted teachings, the lure of passion which youth experience, or the negative influence of scandal, which Jesus said is unavoidable (cf Matthew 18:7).

Left to itself, our fallen human nature tends to follow the law of gravity: it gets pulled down, not up! What lifts us up and strengthens us to resist the downward pull to immorality is God's grace working through the truths of our Catholic Faith!

Now, if these same parents were to speak about the Blessed Mother, especially with a sense of joy, enthusiasm and importance, this is bound to make a deep impact on the child. I have always believed that the initial faith of a child is actually a participation in the faith of the parents, or of other significant people in their lives, such as grandparents, godparents, and teachers. With time, the children will make this participated faith their own personal faith!

What Motivates People to Keep Children from Our Lady?

Through the First Five Saturdays devotion, we make reparation for this failure to teach children about the Blessed Mother due to neglect on the part of parents or others charged with their education. Worse still, however, are those who deliberately sow the seeds of indifference, disrespect, aversion and even contempt for the Blessed Mother. This can result from a number of motives. One would be a deficient religious attitude or prejudice that mistakenly sees Our Lady as one who keeps us from Jesus. A number of our separated brothers and sisters hold the extremely exaggerated notion that Catholics worship Mary or make her into some sort of a "goddess" so that they react to the opposite extreme by minimizing

47

Our Heavenly Father's special predilection for Our Lady by choosing her to be the Mother of His Son! They argue that we must go to Jesus directly, and not to Jesus through Mary!

But how can the one through whom Jesus came into the world and whose last recorded words in Sacred Scripture are, *"Do whatever He tells you"* (John 2:5) ever possibly keep us from Jesus? In our reparation here, we should pray that such persons, who may be quite sincere despite their mistaken idea, may come to see that Mary is an open gate, not a locked door, on the sure path leading to Jesus!

Radical feminists also oppose love and esteem of Our Lady for themselves and others because, as we have seen in previous reflections, they reject certain essential elements of true feminism, namely, virginity and motherhood. They reject virginity because they want no limits on the promiscuous and often perverted sexual freedom they champion.

Motherhood is rejected because it contradicts their desire for pleasure without responsibility, for which reason they are such determined advocates of abortion. Radical feminists fail to see virginity as a precious gift by which youth, before marriage, preserve the gift of their sexuality for the person with whom they will share a lifelong union of love in marriage. They also reject motherhood, the very glory of womanhood, namely, her privilege through union with her husband to cooperate with God in bringing new life into the world!

In contrast, Our Lady is honored by her faithful

children as Virgin and Mother, and as such, she is held up as an example for young people. So as Virgin and Mother, Mary has become for radical feminists an object of distorted teaching, ridicule and even contempt and blasphemy. In their attempts to spread their agenda, they seek to poison the minds and hearts of young people against the Mother of God. Unfortunately, much of the confusion in the Catholic Church today traces back to this source. After all, their mentality is prevalent in our secularized Western society.

The consequence is much like breathing in badly polluted air: it will eventually make one sick. Thus, radical feminist thought has infiltrated the thinking of many Catholic parents and educators, and in turn, like a contagious disease, has been transmitted to a large segment of our Catholic youth, who either do not know Our Lady or are prejudiced against her.

A Bitter Spiritual Battle
Rages to Win the Young

There is a veritable battle between good and evil, light and darkness, going on in the world today! It has always existed, but it seems to have reached epidemic proportions in today's society. This can be especially seen in the struggle to win over the minds and hearts of the young. We saw this with the terrible *"isms"* of the 20th century. Communism broke up families by separating little children from their parents at tender ages, so as to prevent proper moral guidance and religious training by parents, especially in a deeply religious country like Russia. Nazism boasted of its "youth camps" where young people were systematically subjected to an indoctrination that rejected God and glorified a "super race" only to have it end in catastrophic destruction in the world. This spirit is still found today in our post-Christian, secularized society. The media bombards the young with false and immoral values. Just imagine the negative moral effects of MTV on youth not only in America, but throughout the world! Even diplomats, such as at the United Nations, have tried to gain control of the young under the guise of legislating "young peoples' rights." These laws are nothing more than attempts to separate children from parental authority and protection. They would leave children helplessly exposed to all kinds of exploitation by unscrupulous adults!

The Church, led by Pope John Paul II and then by Pope Benedict XVI, is well aware of this unrelenting struggle and its importance. Both sides know that whoever controls the minds and hearts of the young, controls the key to the future! Pope John Paul II, as a young priest in his native Communist-dominated Poland, untiringly reached out to the young to save the nation from embracing atheism.

Despite his poor health, John Paul II used a similar approach for the universal Church through his World Youth Days of prayer, and his successor, Pope Benedict XVI, intends to continue on this course. We, too, will assist in this struggle as we carry out the Five First Saturdays devotion, making reparation for the evil done to our young people and winning the graces of conversion for them, as well as for those who attempt to keep them from coming to Jesus through His Mother!

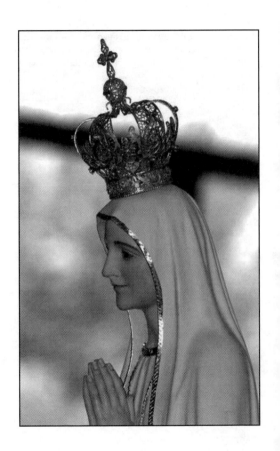

CHAPTER 7
The Fifth Reparation
of the Five First Saturdays

For Those Who Dishonor Our Lady in Her Images

Art plays a very important part in the life of any society. In its many forms, the purpose of art is to give expression to the values, the beauty and the aspirations that humans treasure in their hearts. Art can express many a sentiment from joy to sorrow, hope to disappointment, love to loneliness, even reverence to disrespect. It is one of the primary means by which people of a given generation form and express their culture.

The Powerful Influence of Religious Art
Religious art stands out among all these expressions because it touches the most profound and sacred sentiments we have, namely, those stemming from

our relationship with God. When sacred art genuinely expresses what transpires between God and the individual in the secret depths of his or her heart, it truly lifts up, inspires and enlightens the human spirit. Such art helps us to feel a sense of the presence of God. This in turn moves us to pray more ardently and trust more confidently in His love and providential care. Devout people instinctively know this by their experience.

The Catholic Church has always used art as part of her mission of evangelization. It has always been an important tool for Christian education. In past centuries, when most of the faithful were illiterate, they would learn much about their Catholic Faith by looking at artistic representations of events in Sacred Scripture and the history of the Church. Scenes from the life of Christ, such as those depicting His birth, public life, death, and resurrection, were extremely popular. They made these events of salvation very real and meaningful for these people of simple faith. The same effect continues today when religious art reinforces what a more educated faithful have already studied about the faith.

As Pope John Paul II wrote in his letter to artists in 1999, "In order to communicate the message entrusted to her by Christ, the Church needs art!"

The Image of Our Lady:
A Favorite in Christian Art

Among the most popular images of Catholic art are those of Our Blessed Lady. Without doubt, the theme of the Madonna and Child has inspired some of the most beautiful expressions created by human artists. Even the United States Post Office, despite objections of certain civil libertarians, every Christmas issues its special stamp of the Madonna and Child to meet popular demand.

Special representations of Our Lady have become part of Catholic culture in various countries and even internationally. The image of Our Lady of Guadalupe in Mexico is one of the most outstanding. It was miraculously imprinted on the tilma (a mantle made of cactus fiber) belonging to St. Juan Diego. This tilma, in turn, has been miraculously preserved for nearly five-hundred years.

This image has inspired devotion to Our Lady of Guadalupe as the Queen of the Americas, the Protectress of the Unborn and the Star of Evangelization. Other very popular images of Our Lady include Our Lady of Perpetual Help (Italy), Our Lady of Czestochowa (Poland), Our Lady of Pilar (Spain), Virgin Mary of Kazan (Russia), Our Lady of Walshingham (England) and Our Lady of Loreto (Italy). Over the years, Catholic devotion to Our Lady in these various countries has centered on these images. Many times it was precisely this devotion to Our Lady in these images that preserved a remnant of Catholic culture and identity, especially in times when the Church faced persecution from without and indifference from within.

Devotion to Our Lady through her images has also flourished in connection with places where she has appeared to various members of the faithful over the centuries. Names like Fatima (Portugal), Lourdes and Rue du Bac (France), and Knock (Ireland) are but a few of such places all over the world where the faithful come to honor Our Lady at her shrines. These same faithful and many others keep her image in their homes as reminders of their love for her and of their need to pray to her to seek her motherly protection and intercession.

To Dishonor an Image of Our Lady is a Terrible Offense

Connected to these various images of Our Lady have been certain Marian devotions. These include honoring her joys and sorrows, praying her Rosary, wearing her Miraculous Medal as well as wearing the brown scapular she gave us as Our Lady of Mt. Carmel.

So, when Catholics honor images of Our Lady, there is a considerable sense of piety involved. She is our spiritual Mother who loves and cares for us, our Protectress who defends us from all harm physical and spiritual, our Intercessor with her Son, Jesus Christ.

Therefore, whenever her image is dishonored in any way, it is an offense to devout Catholics because it is a serious dishonor to Our Lady and, consequently, to her Divine Son. It demands reparation for the affront given and intercession for God's mercy for those who caused it!

This Dishonor May Come
from Different Causes

Sometimes this dishonor is shown to Our Lady's images by destroying, mutilating, decapitating, spray painting, burning or in any other way disfiguring them. These are outrages that necessitate our reparation. Many times these things are done by members of occult groups who do them to express their contempt for God. Other times it may be the work of people who are violently angry at God for some distorted reason, and who resort to desecration to convey that anger.

Even very famous images of Our Lady have been disfigured over the centuries. For example, the image of Our Lady of Czestochowa suffered desecration. This sacred image was thought to have been painted by St. Luke on a table top made by St. Joseph and used by the Holy Family at Nazareth. In 1430 a group of robbers (said to be Hussites) attempted to rob this priceless image. They put it onto a wagon to carry it away, but the animals pulling the cart would not move. In desperation, the robbers tried to destroy the image with their swords, inflicting a couple of "wounds" on the face of Our Lady. Interestingly, when certain monks charged with repairing the image later tried to cover the scars on Our Lady's face, the wounds only reappeared.

Consequently, the image still today bears those scars, reminding us of how much indignity is heaped upon Our Lady because she is our spiritual mother! Another example closer to our own day involved the very popular Pieta of Michelangelo in St. Peter's Basilica in Rome which was damaged with hammer blows by a distraught man angry at God.

Another equally outrageous dishonor to Our Lady in her images is to produce distorted images or make them from offensive materials. A blasphemous example of this appeared in an art gallery in Brooklyn, New York. The image of Our Lady was made of a most offensive matter and covered with obscene items! Such outrage is certainly a product of the deliberate contempt and mockery fostered by the atheistic, perverted sub-culture that exists in much of our society today. Such desecrations are terribly offensive to the Lord Jesus because they seriously offend His Mother! No doubt the punishment for these sins will also be great. This is why we need first to make reparation for the offense to Our Lord and His Holy Mother by our loving honor to them, and then pray for those who would produce such disgraceful images.

A final form of dishonor to the images of Our Lady is to forbid them to be displayed for prayer and veneration. This can happen in private homes as well as parish churches. Many churches remodeled after Vatican Council II lost much of their religious art. If you walk into some of these churches today, they resemble stark meeting halls rather than places conducive to fervent prayer and worship. They became subject to what might be called a "neo-iconoclasm," a word stemming from the Greek word for "image-breaking." In the 7th and 8th centuries, especially in the Eastern Church, there was an intense controversy over whether religious images could be used or not. Those who opposed their use said religious images were idols, and so they destroyed them (thus the title "iconoclasts"). The Second Council of Nicea (787) finally defined that religious images were worthy of veneration and ordered them to be restored. After all, they had been part of Christian worship since the earliest centuries of the Church, as paintings in the catacombs attest. In fact, one of the earliest known images of Our Lady is found on the wall of the Roman catacomb known as the Cemetery of St. Priscilla. Art experts estimate it dates back to about AD 175. It shows Our Lady seated, holding the Christ Child on her knee!

We Should Honor Our Lady's Images

We can see how important it is that we honor Our Lady for the dishonors shown her. This is our reparation. Then we must pray for those who have so tragically dishonored her, because they will face a severe judgment for such outrages. These are not usually sins of weakness, but very often involve deliberate contempt. As we practice our devotion of the Five First Saturdays, we will be offering this important reparation and intercession. At the same time, we can do even more. We should have images of Our Lady in our own homes, to remind us of her presence, and of her maternal love and care for our families. We should pray before these images of the Mother of God, especially when we gather with family members to pray her Rosary. We should encourage others to do the same. If you have children or grandchildren that, married or single, have their own homes or apartments, you might get them a favorite picture of Our Lady for Christmas, or on some other special occasion, like their wedding.

Another way to foster honor to Our Lady is to put a statue of her in your yard or on the front lawn. I am sure that many people are as impressed as I am when driving by a home with a religious statue out front that expresses the faith of those who live there.

You might also consider working with others to begin a parish or neighborhood "Pilgrim Virgin of Fatima" program, where the image of Our Lady will travel from home to home or in the parish school from classroom to classroom.

If St. Therese of Lisieux, knowing her mission in Heaven would begin soon, could request that she "Be made known everywhere," how much more would Our Lady want us to do that for her? You will only know in Heaven how many you have helped come closer to the Mother of God and our Mother, too!

SUBSCRIBE TO

SOUL Magazine keeps you updated on the latest news from the World Apostolate of Fatima and the Catholic Church. *SOUL* also carries lively features on faith, prayer, Church history, the lives of the saints, Scripture and Marian devotion. It makes a wonderful gift!

SUBSCRIPTION RATES

(Prices subject to change without notice.)

United States	Canada
1 Year (4 issues) - $13.00	1 Year (4 issues) - $21.00
3 Years (12 issues) - $35.00	3 Years (12 issues) - $60.00

To subscribe, fill out the form below
and mail with your payment to:

SOUL Magazine, Box 976, Washington, NJ 07882

or

Subscribe by phone with your credit card: (866) 513-1917

or

www.wafusa.org

Name _____

Address_____

_____

City_____ State_____ Zip_____

**Now that you know the
Message of Fatima,
why not make a
difference in the world?**

Join the World
Apostolate of Fatima

*Pope John Paul II has said
that the Fatima message is
more relevant today than ever
(Fatima, May 13, 1982) and
that it can be synthesized in
Christ's own words:
"The kingdom of God is at
hand. Repent, and believe in
the Gospel"*
(Vatican City, May 15, 1991)

WRITE: World Apostolate of Fatrima, USA, Box 976,
Washington, NJ 07882
CALL: (908) 689-1700   **WEB:** www.bluearmy.com

- -

**I wish to further the work of Our Lady of Fatima
through the World Aposotlate of Fatima.**

Name _____

Address _____

City _____

State _____ Zip _____

☐ Please send me the Blue Army Pledge and information
about the Apostolate.

☐ Accept my donation of $ _____ to further the work of
the Blue Army.

☐ Please send me information on how to honor Our Lady in
my Will.

First Saturday Aid

The World Apostolate of Fatima, USA

The Blue Army, USA

Washington, New Jersey

www.wafusa.org

(866) 513-1917

In accord with Canon 827 of the New Code of Canon Law, this publication has been submitted to a censor of the Diocese and nothing being found contrary to faith and morals, we hereby grant permission in accord with Canon 824 that it be published.

Rev. Msgr. John B. Szymanski, Vicar General
Diocese of Metuchen, March 15, 2006

N.B. The ecclesiastical permission implies nothing more than the material contained in the publication has been examined by diocesan censors and nothing contrary to faith and morals has been found therein.

2006 Revised Edition

ISBN 1-56036-105-0

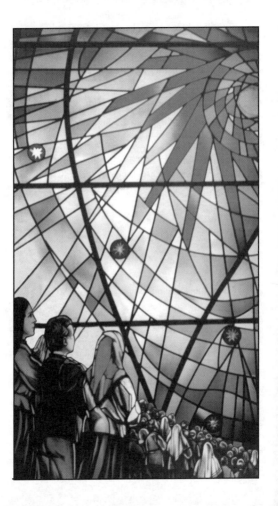

MARY'S GREAT PROMISE
AT FATIMA

Mary, the Mother of God, appeared on earth to offer man the instrument of Divine Mercy – the Holy Rosary – that mighty weapon against the evils of this world which call down the wrath of God.

The place Our Lady chose was the small, rustic, obscure village in Portugal called Fatima. Here, at a site known as the *Cova da Iria*, at high noon on Sunday, May 13, 1917, she appeared to three little shepherds – Lucia, ten years old; Francisco, eight; and Jacinta, seven.

As is the custom after lunch in Portugal, they recited five decades of the Rosary. Finishing their prayers, they began to amuse themselves by building a little house with some loose stones that lay on the ground nearby.

Suddenly, there was a bright flash of lightning in the clear sky. Dreading a thunderstorm, they gathered their flock of sheep to go home.

The children drove their sheep down the hill toward the road. Lightning flashed again as they reached a large holm oak tree. A few steps away, the children were surprised to see a lady all dressed in white, standing just above the branches of a holm oak sapling.

"She was more brilliant than the sun, and radiated a light more clear and intense than a crystal glass filled with sparkling water, when the rays of the burning sun shine through it," Sister Lucia dos Santos wrote of her experience with Our Lady.

"Do not be afraid," the Lady said, "I will do you no harm."

Her indescribably beautiful face was not sad, not happy, but serious. Her hands were clasped before her in prayer with the beads of her rosary hanging down between the fingers of the right hand. Her garments seemed to be made of white light. A mantle covered her head and the simple tunic ran to her feet. The edge of the mantle was of a stronger light which seemed to glitter like gold.

As the children came nearer to her, there followed a dialogue between the Lady and Lucia, during which the Lady invited the children to come to the *Cova* on the thirteenth day of every month until October.

The Ejaculation for Each Decade

There were six apparitions, one on the thirteenth of each month, except in August when the apparition was seen a few days later, at another place, because the children had been imprisoned by the civil authorities.

During these apparitions, Our Lady remained with the children and confided to them a secret which they were not to reveal to anyone. She told them that her home was heaven, asked for the daily recitation of the Rosary and stressed the importance of acts of reparation. She taught them the following ejaculation to be said after each decade:

> *O my Jesus! Forgive us. Save us from the*
> *fire of hell. Lead all souls to heaven,*
> *especially those who are in most need.*

She advised Lucia to learn how to read and write and insisted on the necessity of prayer and sacrifice. She asked the children to accept all suffering in reparation for the numberless sins which offend the Divine Majesty. She ordered that a chapel be built there in her honor and declared that she was the Lady of the Rosary. In 1925, she appeared again to Lucia, repeated the message and promised to aid at the hour of death anyone who would do the following on five consecutive first Saturdays:

The Five First Saturdays
of Reparation to Our Lady

1. Confession *(May be eight days before or after)*.
2. Receive Holy Communion.
3. Recite Five Decades of the Rosary.
4. Meditate on the Mysteries of the Rosary for 15 Minutes.
5. The above exercises should be performed on the first Saturday of five consecutive months with the intention of making reparation to the Immaculate Heart of Mary.

No doubt, at Fatima the Lord wished to inaugurate devotion to her Immaculate Heart – the same way our Lord instituted the nine first Fridays devotion to His Sacred Heart at *Paray-le-Monial*.

During the July 13, 1917 apparition, the Holy Virgin said so kindly and so sadly: "You have seen hell where the souls of poor sinners go. To save them, God wishes to establish in the world devotion to my Immaculate Heart..."

The Five Blasphemies
Against the Immaculate Heart

Our Lord revealed to Sr. Lucia that there are five ways in which people offend and blaspheme against the Immaculate Heart of Mary:

1. Against the Immaculate Conception.
2. Against Her Virginity.
3. Against the Divine Maternity, while refusing to receive Her as the Mother of mankind.

4. By those who try to publicly implant in the hearts of children indifference, disrespect, and even hate against the Immaculate Mother.
5. By those who insult Her directly in Her Sacred Images.

The Great Promise

Our Blessed Lady promised to Sister Lucia on December 10, 1925:

"Look, my daughter, at my Heart, surrounded with thorns with which ungrateful men pierce me every moment by their blasphemies and ingratitude. You at least try to console me and say that I promise to assist at the hour of death, with the graces necessary for salvation, all those who, on the first Saturday of five consecutive months, shall confess, receive Holy Communion, recite five decades of the Rosary, and keep me company for 15 minutes while meditating on the 15[1] mysteries of the Rosary, with the intention of making reparation to me."

The Words of Jesus on the
Five First Saturdays Devotion

February 15, 1926 - The Child Jesus to Sr. Lucia concerning the devotion of the consecutive Five First Saturdays:

"It is true, my daughter, that many souls begin the First Saturdays, but few finish them, and those who do complete them do so in order to receive the graces that are promised thereby. It would please me more if they did Five with fervor and with the intention of making reparation to the Heart of your heavenly Mother, than if they did Fifteen, in a tepid and indifferent manner..."

---

1 Pope John Paul II added the Luminous Mysteries.

5

MEDITATIONS ON THE TWENTY MYSTERIES

For The Five First Saturdays of Reparation to The Immaculate Heart of Mary

(Meditation on the mysteries is the most important part of the Rosary. Put yourself in the presence of Jesus or Mary and live the mysteries with them.)

Prayer to Our Lady of Fatima

Most Holy Virgin, you came to Fatima to reveal to three little children the treasure of graces hidden in the recitation of the Rosary. Inspire my heart with a sincere love of this devotion so that, by meditating on the mysteries of our redemption that it recalls, I may gather the fruits and obtain the special grace which I ask of you during these fifteen minutes for the greater glory of God, for your honor, and for the good of souls. Amen.

THE FIVE JOYFUL MYSTERIES

The Annunciation
Luke 1:26-38

Let us consider in this mystery – how the Angel Gabriel was sent from God to a town called Nazareth to a virgin, whose name was Mary, and who was betrothed to a man named Joseph. And when the angel had come to her, he said: "Hail, full of grace, the Lord is with thee. Blessed art thou among women."

When Mary had heard these words she was troubled, and kept pondering what manner of greeting this might be.

But the angel drew near and said to her, "Do not be afraid, Mary, for you have found favor with God. Behold, you will conceive in your womb and bear a son, and you shall name him Jesus. He will be great and will be called Son of the Most High."

And Mary said to the angel: "How can this be, since I have no relations with a man?"

And the angel answered and said to her, "The Holy Spirit will come upon you, and the power of the Most High will overshadow you. Therefore the child to be born will be called holy, the Son of God. And behold, Elizabeth, your relative, has also conceived a son in her old age, and this is the sixth month for her who was called barren; for nothing will be impossible for God."

Mary, bowing her head in humility, answered: "Behold, I am the handmaid of the Lord. May it be done to me according to your word." And the angel departed from her.

Prayer: *Immaculate Heart of Mary, by the message of an Angel, the Holy Spirit overshadowed you. Your most pure and virginal womb became the sacramental tabernacle sheltering the Son of God. At Fatima, the Angel of Portugal came with a message for the three shepherd children to prepare them for your heavenly visit: "Do not be afraid! I am the Angel of Peace. Pray with me: My God, I believe, I adore, I hope, and I love You! I ask pardon of You for those who do not believe, do not adore, do not hope, and do not love You." Help me to pray and live the Angel's prayer at Fatima.*

Recite: *Our Father, once; Hail Mary, ten times Glory be to the Father, once; and O my Jesus, once.*

The Visitation
Luke 1:39-56

Let us consider in this mystery – how the Blessed Virgin Mary arose and went into the hill country, to a town of Judah, to visit her cousin Elizabeth, who, in her old age, was soon to give birth to Saint John the Baptist.

No sooner did Mary enter into the house than Elizabeth, filled with the Holy Spirit, cried out with a loud voice saying, "Most blessed are you among women, and blessed is the fruit of your womb. And how does this happen to me, that the mother of my Lord should come to me? For at the moment the sound of your greeting reached my ears, the infant in my womb leaped for joy. Blessed are you who believed that what was spoken to you by the Lord would be fulfilled."

Whereupon Mary replied with that canticle of canticles, *The Magnificat*.

The Magnificat

*My soul proclaims the greatness of the Lord, my spirit
   rejoices in God my Savior.*
*For he has looked upon his handmaid's lowliness; behold
   from now on will all ages call me blessed.*
*The Mighty One has done great things for me, and holy is
   his Name.*
His mercy is from age to age to those who fear him.

He has shown might with his arm, dispersed the arrogant of mind and heart.

He has thrown down the rulers from their thrones, but lifted up the lowly.

The hungry he has filled with good things, the rich he has sent away empty.

He has helped Israel his servant, remembering his mercy according to his promise to our fathers, to Abraham and to his descendants forever.

Prayer: *Immaculate Heart of Mary, your visit to your cousin, Elizabeth, filled her heart with song and praise. At Fatima, you visited the three little shepherds. They, too, were captured by your love: "Do not be afraid. I will do you no harm. Pray the Rosary every day, in order to obtain peace for the world, and the end of the war." "When you pray the Rosary, say after each mystery: O my Jesus, forgive us, save us from the fire of hell. Lead all souls to Heaven, especially those who are most in need." Abide in my heart, also, and grant me the grace to remain faithful to your Rosary.*

Recite: *Our Father, once; Hail Mary, ten times; Glory be to the Father, once; and O my Jesus, once.*

The Nativity
Luke 2:1-19

Let us consider in this mystery – how Joseph and his wife, Mary, who was with Child, went to Bethlehem, the city of David, to register according to a decree sent out by the Roman emperor commanding a census of the whole world.

And it came to pass while they were there that the days for Mary to be delivered were fulfilled. But there was no room for them at the inn. Therefore, they took shelter in a stable where she brought forth her first born son and laid Him in a manger. This was the first Christmas.

A multitude of heavenly hosts sang: "Glory to God in the highest and on earth peace to those on whom His favor rests."

Shepherds came to adore the newborn king. And all who heard marveled at the things told by the shepherds. But Mary kept in mind all those things, pondering them in her heart.

Prayer: *Immaculate Heart of Mary, heaven's angels sang in jubilation to witness the birth of Our Lord. The shepherds knelt at the manger. Soon after the great star gleamed in the sky guiding the Magi. At Fatima, you promised a miracle for all to believe. The clouds parted on October 13th, and the great solar star danced through the heav-*

ens, once again showering favors of light upon the earth. Abide with me as I pray the interior prayer the little shepherds received in their hearts as they fell to their knees: "O Most Holy Trinity, I adore You!
My God, my God, I love You in the most Blessed Sacrament!"

Recite: *Our Father*, once; *Hail Mary*, ten times; *Glory be to the Father*, once; and *O my Jesus*, once.

The Presentation
Luke 2:22-39

Let us consider in this mystery – how the Blessed Virgin Mary, on the day of her purification, together with her husband Joseph, took Jesus up to the Temple in Jerusalem to present him to the Lord. They carried with them a pair of young turtledoves, an offering which the poorest were obliged to make.

Now, there was in Jerusalem a devout man named Simeon. It had been revealed to this just and devout man by the Holy Spirit that he should not see death before he had seen the Messiah.

And he came by the inspiration of the Spirit into the Temple at the time when Mary and Joseph brought in the Child Jesus.

Simeon took the Child in his arms and blessed God saying: "Now, Master, you may let your servant go in peace, according to your word, for my eyes have seen your salvation, which you prepared in the sight of all the peoples, a light for revelation to the Gentiles, and glory for your people Israel."

Joseph and Mary marveled at the things spoken concerning Him. Simeon blessed the Holy Family, and said to Mary, "Behold, this child is destined for the fall and rise of many in Israel, and to be a sign that will be contradicted (and you yourself a sword will pierce) so that the thoughts of many hearts may be revealed."

And when they had fulfilled all things as prescribed in the Law, they returned to Nazareth.

Prayer: *Immaculate Heart of Mary, your Holy Family fulfilled all precepts of the law with profound humility and God's favored blessing, yet your own soul was to be pierced by a sword. Your words to Sr. Lucia grieve me deeply: "Look, my daughter, at my heart surrounded with thorns..." It is my great desire to console you and remove these thorns. I pray that your words to Sr. Lucia may be applied to me: "You, at least, try to console me..."*

Recite: *Our Father,* once; *Hail Mary,* ten times; *Glory be to the Father,* once; and *O my Jesus,* once.

The Finding of the Child in the Temple
Luke 2:41-52

Let us consider in this mystery — how the Blessed Virgin Mary, when Jesus was twelve years old, took Him to Jerusalem according to the custom of the Feast of the Passover. And after they had fulfilled the days, when they were returning, the boy Jesus remained in Jerusalem, and His parents did not know it.

But thinking that He was in the caravan, they had come a day's journey before it occurred to them to look for Him among their relatives and friends.

And they sought Him for a space of three days, and found Him in the Temple, sitting in the midst of the teachers, disputing with them. And all who were listening to Him were amazed at His answers.

And when Joseph and Mary saw Him they were astonished. And His mother said to Him, "Son, why have you done this to us? Your father and I have been looking for you with great anxiety."

And He said to them, "Why were you looking for me? Did you not know that I must be in my Father's house?"

He arose and returned with His parents to Nazareth, and was subject to them. And Jesus advanced in wisdom and age and grace before God and men.

Prayer: *Immaculate Heart of Mary, what joy filled your heart upon finding Him in the Temple. Intercede for me with your Divine Child that I may remain always faithful to the Church and never lose Jesus through mortal sin. If I should offend Him, may I seek the Sacrament of Reconciliation immediately with a contrite heart. I pray for the grace to respond to your request at Fatima: "Are you willing to offer yourselves to God and bear all the sufferings He wills to send you, as an act of reparation for the sins by which He is offended, and of supplication for the conversion of sinners? Then you are going to have much to suffer, but the grace of God will be your comfort."*

Recite: *Our Father,* once; *Hail Mary,* ten times; *Glory be to the Father,* once; and *O my Jesus,* once.

THE FIVE LUMINOUS MYSTERIES

The Baptism in the Jordan
Matthew 3:1-17

Let us consider in this mystery – how John the Baptist was preaching a baptism of repentance for the forgiveness of sins.

Jesus came from Galilee to the Jordan River to be baptized. Upon seeing Him, John declared that Jesus should be the one baptizing him, not John baptizing Jesus. Yet Jesus assured him that it was proper to be done this way.

After being baptized, Jesus came out of the water and immediately the heavens opened and the Spirit of God descended upon Him in the form of a dove.

Then a loud voice from heaven was heard, saying, "This is my beloved Son, with whom I am well pleased."

Prayer: *Immaculate Heart of Mary, your beloved Son did not have to be baptized for He was God Himself. For this great act of humility, God voiced His profound pleasure. At Fatima, you*

*revealed to the three little shepherds that God
was pleased with their sacrifices. I offer myself
to you, for your promise at Fatima:*

*"My Immaculate Heart will be your refuge
and the way that will lead you to God." May
your Immaculate Heart be my refuge so that
my every thought, word, and deed may be pleasing to God.*

Recite: *Our Father, once; Hail Mary, ten times;
Glory be to the Father, once; and
O my Jesus, once.*

The Wedding at Cana
John 2:1-11

Let us consider in this mystery – how a marriage
occurred at Cana of Galilee. Jesus and His disciples
were in attendance along with Our Blessed Mother.

When the wine began to run out, Mary told this
to her Divine Son. He reminded her that the time
for His ministry had not yet come. She urged the
attendants to do whatever He told them.

There were six stone jars nearby that each held
about 20 or 30 gallons. He instructed them to fill the
jars with water to the brim. The attendants did as He
said. Then Jesus told them to draw some of the
water out and bring it to the chief steward. The
steward did not know where it came from but tast-

ed the water turned into wine. He then called the bridegroom, telling him that usually the good wine is served first. Then, after the guests had drunk freely, the poor wine is served. Yet he had kept the good wine until now. This was Christ's first public miracle.

Prayer: *Immaculate Heart of Mary, Jesus changed water into wine at your request. Your gracious concern for others is never-ending. As Bridegroom of the Church, Jesus revealed His glory and gave proof that He was the Messiah. At Fatima, the great Miracle of the Sun was proof of your promise. With Lucia I ask: "What do you want of me?"*

As at Cana, I abide to your request: "Do whatever He tells you."

Please pray with me, Mother. Sanctify me so I may bring others to God.

Recite: *Our Father,* once; *Hail Mary,* ten times; *Glory be to the Father,* once; and *O my Jesus,* once.

The Proclamation of The Kingdom of God
Luke 10:1-12

Let us consider in this mystery – how Jesus, after fasting forty days in the desert, traveled through the towns and villages of Galilee, proclaiming His message of belief in the gospel and repentance.

He declared that the time of fulfillment was now, and the Kingdom of Heaven was at hand. He charged the disciples to go forth to preach thus, and if they were rejected to leave that place and move on.

He warned them that He was sending them out like sheep among wolves. But He also encouraged them not to fear the opposition, because the Holy Spirit would give them the words as they proclaimed the Kingdom of Heaven on earth.

Prayer: *Immaculate Heart of Mary, you requested of Sr. Lucia that the Five First Saturdays devotion be promoted for the conversion of sinners and a means of salvation: "I promise to assist at the hour of death, with the graces necessary for salvation, all those who, on the First Saturday of five consecutive months, shall confess, receive Holy Communion, recite five decades of the Rosary, and keep me company for fifteen minutes while meditating on the fifteen mysteries of the Rosary, with the intention of making reparation to me." I realize by your words, "keep me company," that you truly are present when I respond to your request.*

Recite: *Our Father*, once; *Hail Mary*, ten times; *Glory be to the Father*, once; and *O my Jesus*, once.

The Transfiguration
Mark 9:2-8

Let us consider in this mystery – how Jesus took Peter, James and John up a high mountain to pray.

While He was praying, His face changed its appearance and His garments became dazzling white. Then two men appeared, who conversed with Him – they were Moses and Elijah.

They spoke to Him about His forthcoming Passion and death in Jerusalem. The three apostles witnessed all that was happening and Peter told Jesus it was good that they were there. He offered to build three booths, one for Jesus and one each for Moses and Elijah, not knowing what he was saying. Then a cloud overshadowed them, and the three apostles were very afraid. A voice from the cloud told them that this was His Beloved Son and to listen to Him. Then Jesus came and told them to rise and not to be afraid. When they raised their heads, Jesus was alone.

Prayer: *Immaculate Heart of Mary, your appearance to the little shepherds at Fatima "was more brilliant than the sun." Opening your hands, you communicated by a reflection emanating from them, a light so intimate, penetrating their hearts to the depths of their souls, enabling them to see themselves in God, "God who was that light." Francisco declared: "But what filled me with the greatest joy of all was to see God in this light*

which Our Lady was directing into our hearts."
Please direct my ways, Mother, so my heart may
be filled with God.

Recite: *Our Father*, once; *Hail Mary*, ten times;
Glory be to the Father, once; and
O my Jesus, once.

The Institution of the Eucharist
Luke 22:14-20

Let us consider in this mystery – how at the Last
Supper Christ gave Himself to us.

He took the bread, blessed it and gave it to His
apostles saying "This is my body, which is given for
you." Next, He took the cup of wine and said it was
the new covenant in His blood, which was to be
shed on behalf of many for the forgiveness of sins.
Here, Christ declares the old covenant with Moses is
now replaced with a new covenant. He leaves us His
Body and Blood for all generations to share.

Prayer: *Immaculate Heart of Mary, the great gift of*
the Holy Eucharist, the Real Presence of Jesus,
was communicated to the three little shepherds.
The Angel appeared for the third time holding a
chalice in his left hand, with a Host suspended
above it, from which some drops of blood fell
into the sacred chalice. Kneeling he prayed "Most
Holy Trinity, Father, Son, and Holy Spirit, I

*adore you profoundly and I offer You the most
precious Body, Blood, Soul and Divinity of
Jesus Christ, present in all the tabernacles of the
world, in reparation for the outrages, sacrileges,
and indifference by which He is offended..."* I
beg you, dear Mother, please flood my soul with
an increase of faith.

Recite: *Our Father,* once; *Hail Mary,* ten times;
Glory be to the Father, once; and
O my Jesus, once.

THE FIVE SORROWFUL MYSTERIES

The Agony in the Garden
Matthew 26:36-46

Let us consider in this mystery – how on Holy Thursday after Jesus had instituted the Holy Eucharist, accompanied by His disciples, He went to Mount Olivet, where there was a garden called Gethsemane.

And He said to them, "My soul is sorrowful even to death. Remain here and keep watch with me." Then falling upon His face, He prayed, saying: "My Father, if it is possible, let this cup pass from me; yet, not as I will but as you will."

Thus Jesus prayed three times, and fell into an agony and His sweat became as drops of blood, trickling down to the ground. And there appeared an angel, who strengthened Him. Then Jesus arose, found His disciples asleep and said to them: "Are you still sleeping and taking your rest? Behold, the hour is at hand when the Son of Man is to be handed over to sinners. Get up, let us go. Look, my betrayer is at hand."

Prayer: *Immaculate Heart of Mary, by the overwhelming anguish and grief Our Savior suffered in His Agony, I pray for the grace to respond to your request at Fatima: "Sacrifice yourselves for sinners, and say many times, especially whenever you make some sacrifice: O Jesus, it is for love of You, for the conversion of sinners, and in reparation for the sins committed against the Immaculate Heart of Mary."*

Recite: *Our Father*, once; *Hail Mary*, ten times; *Glory be to the Father*, once; and *O my Jesus*, once.

The Scourging at the Pillar
Luke 23:1-22 and John 19:1

Let us consider in this mystery – how, in the early morning, Jesus was led before the Roman Governor, Pontius Pilate, to be tried.

But Pilate knew that Jesus had been delivered by the envy of the priests and Pharisees and He said to them: "You brought this man to me and accused him of inciting the people to revolt. I have conducted my investigation in your presence and have not found this man guilty of the charges you have brought against him, nor did Herod, for he sent him back to us. So no capital crime has been committed by him. Therefore, I shall have him flogged and then release him."

Jesus was then led away, stripped of His garments and tied to a pillar, where He was most inhumanly scourged by cruel executioners.

His Precious Blood streamed from His flesh mangled by so many blows.

Prayer: *Immaculate Heart of Mary, Jesus suffered this inhuman punishment to atone for the sins of man. You revealed to Jacinta that many souls go to hell because of sins of the flesh. Grant me the virtue of purity so I may never cause myself or my neighbor the loss of heaven. May the words of Jacinta become my own: "But I offer everything for sinners, and in reparation to the Immaculate Heart of Mary…{Our Lord and our Lady} greatly love those who suffer for the conversion of sinners."*

Recite: *Our Father*, once; *Hail Mary*, ten times; *Glory be to the Father*, once; and *O my Jesus*, once.

The Crowning with Thorns
Matthew 27:26-31

Let us consider in this mystery – how, after Jesus had been scourged, Pilate delivered Him up to be crucified.

The soldiers of the procurator took Jesus into the praetorium and gathered together about Him the whole cohort.

And they stripped Him of His garments and put on Him a scarlet cloak; and plaiting a crown of thorns, they put it upon His head, and a reed into His right hand; and bending the knee before Him they mocked Him, saying "Hail, King of the Jews!" Others spat on Him, and took the reed and struck His head.

At last, they blindfolded Him and renewed all manner of insult and injury.

Prayer: *Immaculate Heart of Mary, at Tuy, Sr. Lucia was blessed to see the Trinity, with Jesus Crucified, above the altar. His Precious drops of Blood were spilling into His chalice. From His side, rivers of water spilled forth over the altar with the words, 'Graces and Mercy.' Your Immaculate Heart was there, also. I pray, be with me as I approach the altar that I may receive worthily His grace and mercy, remembering the words of the Angel at*

Fatima: "Take and drink the body and blood of Jesus Christ, horribly outraged by ungrateful men! Make reparation for their crimes and console your God."

Recite: *Our Father*, once; *Hail Mary*, ten times; *Glory be to the Father*, once; and *O my Jesus*, once.

The Carrying of the Cross
Mark 15:20-26

Let us consider in this mystery — how the soldiers seized Jesus, removed His scarlet cloak and put on His own garments.

A heavy cross is placed upon His bleeding shoulder and He is led away to be crucified. Each step on this agonizing journey causes terrific pain throughout His torn body. The cross cut deeply into His wounded shoulder. He struggled along to Calvary, stumbling and falling beneath the heavy weight of the cross amidst the shouts and jeers of His own people. Finally, they came to a place called *Golgotha*, that is, the Place of the Skull.

Prayer: *Immaculate Heart of Mary, with compassion I recall how painful it must have been for you to see Jesus suffering for the sins of man. Inspire* *me with a keen sorrow for my past sins. In moments of trial, may I remember your promise: "Are you suffering a great deal? Do not lose hope, I will not forsake you." Your words to the three little shepherds bring forth your maternal concern for me: "Do not offend the Lord anymore, because He is already so much offended." I desire never to offend God again.*

Recite: *Our Father*, once; *Hail Mary*, ten times; *Glory be to the Father*, once; and *O my Jesus*, once.

The Crucifixion
Luke 23:33-46 and John 19:16-30

Let us consider in this mystery – how, when Jesus reached the top of Mount Calvary, He was stripped of His garments and then cruelly nailed to the cross.

Then two robbers were crucified with Him, one on His right hand and one on His left. And the people mocked Jesus, saying: "He saved others, let him save himself if he is the chosen one, the Messiah of God."

Jesus spoke: "Father forgive them, for they know not what they do."

One of the thieves who was crucified with Him

blasphemed Jesus saying: "Are you not the Messiah? Save yourself and us."

But the other rebuked him and exclaimed: "Have you no fear of God, for you are subject to the same condemnation? And indeed, we have been condemned justly, for the sentence we received corresponds to our crimes, but this man has done nothing criminal." Then he said: "Jesus, remember me when you come into your kingdom."

Jesus answered: "Amen, I say to you, today you will be with me in Paradise."

Then Jesus looked down from His cross and beheld His Mother, Mary, and John, His beloved disciple. Jesus said to His Mother: "Woman, behold your son." And to John, He said, "Behold your mother." From that hour John took the mother of Jesus to himself, as if she were his own mother.

And when the sixth hour came, there was darkness over the whole land until the ninth hour. And at the ninth hour Jesus cried out in a loud voice, saying: "My God, My God, why have you forsaken me?"

Soon afterward Jesus exclaimed: "I thirst." Then a soldier took a sponge soaked in common wine, put it on a reed and gave it to Him to drink. After He had taken the wine Jesus said: "It is finished." Then He cried out in a loud voice: "Father, into your hands I commend My spirit." He then bowed His head and died.

Prayer: *Immaculate Heart of Mary, for the sake of the bitter anguish you suffered at the foot of the cross, help me to be charitable to all who offend me and to offer and make sacrifices in supplication for the conversion of sinners. At Fatima, you showed the three shepherd children a vision of hell: "You have seen hell where the souls of poor sinners go...." Grant me the grace to overcome evil in moments of temptation, especially at my last hour. Your words to Sr. Lucia sustain me: "I promise to assist at the hour of death, with the graces necessary for salvation, all those who, on the first Saturday of five consecutive months...."*

Recite: *Our Father, once; Hail Mary, ten times; Glory be to the Father, once; and O my Jesus, once.*

THE FIVE GLORIOUS MYSTERIES

The Resurrection
Matthew 28:1-7

Let us consider in this mystery – how, as the morning of the third day dawned, Our Lord Jesus Christ rose from the dead, and came forth from the grave in all His glory.

At the same time, there was a great earthquake. An angel of the Lord came down from heaven, rolled away the stone from the sepulchre and sat upon it. His countenance was as lightning and His garments white as snow. When the guards saw the angel, they were struck with terror and fell to the ground as if they were dead.

Meanwhile, three pious women brought spices, that they might anoint the body of Jesus. But when they came to the sepulchre they saw that it was empty. And the angel said to them: "Do not be afraid! I know that you are seeking Jesus the cruci-fied. He is not here, for He has been raised just as He said. Come and see the place where He lay. Then go quickly and tell His disciples, 'He has been raised from the dead, and He is going before you to Galilee; there you will see Him.' Behold, I have told you."

Prayer: *Immaculate Heart of Mary, the angel announced to three pious women who came to anoint Our Lord, "Do not be afraid!...." At Fatima, the angel prepared the three shepherd children to see God with the same greeting: "Do not be afraid." It is my desire to keep company with those pleasing to God, so I, too, may hear the words, "Do not be afraid" when I see Him in His Glory. Please grant me the grace to avoid all occasions of sin.*

Recite: *Our Father*, once; *Hail Mary*, ten times; *Glory be to the Father*, once; and *O my Jesus*, once.

The Ascension
Matthew 28:18-20 and Acts 1:9-12

Let us consider in this mystery – how on the fortieth day Jesus appeared to his eleven apostles for the last time in the upper room at Jerusalem.

He ate with them and told them to wait in Jerusalem until they would receive the Holy Spirit. And He said to them: "All power in heaven and on earth has been given to me. Go, therefore, and make disciples of all nations, baptizing them in the name of the Father, and of the Son, and of the Holy Spirit, teaching them to observe all that I have commanded you. And behold, I am with you always, until the end of the age."

Then He went with His apostles to Mount Olivet. Here, He raised his hands and blessed them. And it came to pass that, while He blessed them, He began to ascend, and was raised to heaven. The apostles adored Him and looked after Jesus, until a cloud hid Him from their sight.

But as they were looking after Him, two angels appeared to them, and said: "Men of Galilee, why are you standing there looking at the sky? This Jesus who has been taken up from you into heaven will return in the same way as you have seen Him going into heaven." The apostles rejoiced at these tidings, and they went forth and preached, while the Lord worked with them and confirmed the preaching by the signs that followed.

Prayer: *Immaculate Heart of Mary, you fulfilled your promise in October to perform a miracle. The clouds parted in heaven and the little shepherds were graced to see you with St. Joseph who was holding the Child Jesus in his arms. It is my great desire to go to Heaven, yet I realize by your words for blessed Francisco how deficient I am! "He [Francisco] will go there [Heaven] too, but*

he must say many Rosaries." I pray, dear
Mother, for the gift of prayer and self-denial, so
I may attend to the Angel at Fatima: "What
are you doing? Pray, pray very much! The most
Holy Hearts of Jesus and Mary have designs of
mercy on you. Offer prayers and sacrifices con-
stantly to the Most High!"

Recite: *Our Father*, once; *Hail Mary*, ten times;
                 Glory be to the Father, once; and
                 O my Jesus, once.

The Descent of The Holy Spirit
upon the Apostles
Acts 2:1-47

Let us consider in this mystery – when the days of Pentecost were drawing to a close, the apostles, disciples and Mary, the Mother of Jesus, were again assembled together in the upper room.

And suddenly on the tenth day there came a sound from heaven, as of a mighty rushing wind, and it filled the whole house where they were sitting.

There appeared to them parted tongues as of fire, which settled upon each one of them, and they were filled with the Holy Spirit, and began to speak in diverse tongues.

Now there were staying at Jerusalem, Jews and devout men from every nation under the heaven.

And when this sound was heard the multitude gathered and were bewildered in mind, because each heard them speaking in his own language.

They were all amazed and marveled, saying: "Are not all these people who are speaking Galilean? Then how does each of us hear them in his own native language? We are Parthians, Medes, and Elamites, inhabitants of Mesopotamia, Judea and Cappadocia, Pontus and Asia, Phrygia and Pamphylia, Egypt and the districts of Libya near Cyrene, as well as travelers from Rome, both Jews and converts to Judaism, Cretans and Arabs, yet we hear them speaking in our own tongues of the mighty acts of God."

Peter stood forth, and said: "Repent and be baptized, every one of you, in the name of Jesus Christ for the forgiveness of your sins; and you will receive the gift of the Holy Spirit. For the promise is made to you and to your children and to all those far off, whomever the Lord our God will call."

Many believed and were baptized; and the same day about three thousand were received into the Church.

Prayer: *Immaculate Heart of Mary, Sr. Lucia received lights concerning the Holy Trinity which she was not permitted to reveal. It is my heartfelt desire to obtain the virtues necessary to be pleasing to God. Please ask the Holy Spirit Whom Christ*

promised to His apostles and to the world, the
gift of fortitude that I may have the courage to
be diligent in the pursuit of knowledge and hon-
est in its use. Enlighten my understanding, make
me prudent in my undertakings, courageous in
adversity and humble in prosperity. I join with
the little shepherds in their prayer "O most Holy
Trinity, I adore you! My God, my God, I love
You in the most Blessed Sacrament!"

Recite:　*Our Father*, once;　*Hail Mary*, ten times;
Glory be to the Father, once; and
O my Jesus, once.

The Assumption
Revelation 12:1-6

Let us consider in this mystery – how the Blessed Virgin Mary, preserved by a singular privilege from the stain of original sin, was also exempt from that common curse on sinful man, "For you are dirt, and unto dirt you shall return." (Gen. 3:19)

God would not permit her virginal body, from which His own Son took human form, to return to dust. It was the Almighty's wish that her mortal body be assumed into heaven to be reunited with her most pure soul amid the highest demonstrations of jubilee and triumph.

Prayer: *Immaculate Heart of Mary, your appearance above the Cova Tree caused many to question the sincerity of the three little shepherds. However, even nature responded to your grace, for the little branch upon which you stood assumed your heavenly fragrance. I pray for the grace to be emptied of myself so I, too, may be assumed by your holy fragrance. I realize it was through their purity they were blessed to see you "ascend toward the east," into the heavens.*

Recite: *Our Father,* once; *Hail Mary,* ten times; *Glory be to the Father,* once; and *O my Jesus,* once.

The Coronation
Judith 15:9-10

Let us consider in this mystery – how the Glorious Virgin Mary, upon entering the Kingdom of Heaven, was greeted by her Divine Son who placed her by the heavenly throne of the Most Holy Trinity. Exalted above all the choirs of angels, He crowned her before the court of Heaven with the diadem of eternal glory.

At that moment Mary, the Mother of Jesus, is clearly seen as the great Mediatrix of Graces, the lover of mankind, the Refuge of Sinners.

Prayer: *Immaculate Heart of Mary, yours is truly a pilgrim heart. The words of Pope Pius XII ring true today and give perpetual reverence to your name: "Since I crowned Our Lady Queen of the world, she has gone forth like a pilgrim virgin. And the graces and miracles….she has performed along the way are such that we can hardly believe what we are seeing with our own eyes." As Queen of all Hearts, please bless my path and lead me in the ways of God.*

Recite: *Our Father*, once; *Hail Mary*, ten times
Glory be to the Father, once; and
One *O my Jesus*, once.

PRAYERS AT THE CONCLUSION
OF THE ROSARY

Hail, Holy Queen

Hail, Holy Queen, Mother of Mercy, our life, our sweetness and our hope. To thee do we cry, poor banished children of Eve. To thee do we send up our sighs, mourning and weeping in this valley of tears.

Turn then, most gracious advocate, thine eyes of mercy towards us; and after this, our exile, show unto us the blessed fruit of thy womb, Jesus. O clement, O loving, O sweet Virgin Mary!

R. *Pray for us, O most holy Mother of God.*

V. *That we may be worthy of the promises of Christ.*

Let us Pray:

O God, Whose only begotten Son, by his life, death and resurrection, has purchased for us the rewards of eternal life; grant we beseech Thee, that meditating on these mysteries of the most Holy Rosary of the Blessed Virgin Mary, we may imitate what they contain, and obtain what they promise. Through the same Christ, Our Lord. Amen.

Prayer for the Intention
of the Holy Father

Our Father, once;
Hail Mary, once;
and *Glory Be,* once. *Amen.*

Prayer of Consecration

Vouchsafe to reign, O most loving Mother,
over this family, that it may be your own, and over
each one of us who is, and wishes to be, yours in
prosperity and in adversity, in joy and in sorrow, in
health and in sickness, in life and in death.
Reign over our wills, leading them in the path of
virtue traced by you for us with your example, in a
perfect submission to the will of God.

Reign in our hearts which desire nothing but to be
consumed with love for you and Jesus. We want to be
pure like you; we want to atone for so many crimes
committed against you and against Jesus.

Bring to our country and to the whole world the
kingdom of peace in justice and charity.

Therefore, we now promise to imitate your virtues
in the practice of a Christian life, and to offer you
the wreath of our Rosary and the flowers of our
sacrifices, in the spirit of Reparation and Penance.

PRAYERS FROM FATIMA

The prayers taught at Fatima are simple in structure, profound in depth. To a world poor and needy in Faith and Charity these prayers stress ancient Truths of our Holy Catholic Church – especially concerning the Holy Eucharist and Mary, the Immaculate Mother of God.

Pardon Prayer

My God, I believe, I adore, I hope, and I love You! I beg pardon for those who do not believe, do not adore, do not hope, and do not love You.

Sacrifice Prayer

Our Lady requested this prayer be said many times, especially whenever we make some sacrifice:

O Jesus, it is for love of You, for the conversion of sinners, and in reparation for the sins committed against the Immaculate Heart of Mary.

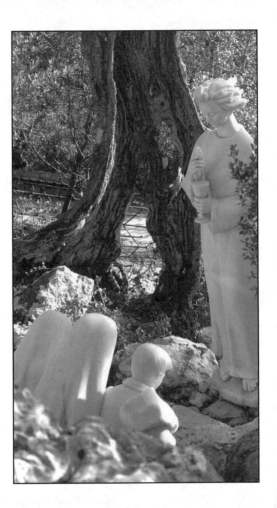

Eucharistic Prayer

This prayer stresses that most beautiful truth – the all-powerful, all-loving God upon our very altars.

Most Holy Trinity, I adore You! My God, My God, I love You in the Most Blessed Sacrament.

The Angel's Prayer

With the Blessed Sacrament suspended in the air, the angel at Fatima prostrated himself, and recited the prayer:

Most Holy Trinity, Father, Son and Holy Spirit, I adore You profoundly, and I offer You the most precious Body, Blood, Soul, and Divinity of Jesus Christ, present in all the tabernacles of the world, in reparation for the outrages, sacrileges and indifference with which He Himself is offended. And, through the infinite merits of His most Sacred Heart, and the Immaculate Heart of Mary, I beg of You the conversion of poor sinners.

The Decade Prayer

O my Jesus! Forgive us, save us from the fire of hell. Lead all souls to heaven, especially those who are most in need.

Prayer for the Canonization of Blessed Francisco and Jacinta

Most Holy Trinity, Father, Son and Holy Spirit, I adore you profoundly and I thank You for the apparitions of the Most Holy Virgin of Fatima.

By the infinite merits of the Sacred Heart of Jesus and through the intercession of the Immaculate Heart of Mary I implore you - if it should be for Your greater glory and the good of our souls - to glorify in the sight of Your Holy Church Blessed Francisco and Jacinta, granting us through their intercession the grace which we implore. Amen.

Recite: *Our Father*, once;
             Hail Mary, ten times; and
             Glory be to the Father, once.

SISTER LUCIA ON THE
IMPORTANCE OF THE ROSARY

Reprinted from
Calls from the Message of Fatima
by Lucia of Jesus and of the Immaculate Heart

And Our Lady ended her Message on that 13th
May 1917 with the words: "Pray the Rosary every
day, in order to obtain peace for the world, and
the end of the war."

Why should Our Lady have told us to say the
Rosary every day rather than telling us to go to
Mass every day?

This is a question that I have been asked many
times, and it is one which I should like to reply to
here. I cannot be absolutely certain of the answer,
as Our Lady did not explain, and it never occurred
to me to ask. Hence, I say only what I think, and
what I have come to understand about it all. In
fact, I willingly leave all interpretation of the
meaning of the Message to Holy Church, because
it pertains to the Church to do so; hence, I
humbly and willingly submit myself to whatever It

may wish to say or to correct, amend or declare.

As regards the question referred to above, I think that God is Father; and as Father He adapts Himself to the needs and possibilities of his children. Now, if God, through Our Lady, had asked us to go to Mass and receive Holy Communion every day, there would undoubtedly have been a great many people who would have said, quite rightly, that this was not possible. Some, on account of the distance separating them from the nearest church where Mass was celebrated; others on account of the circumstances of their lives, their state in life, their job, the state of their health, etc. On the other hand, to pray the Rosary is something everybody can do, rich and poor, wise and ignorant, great and small.

All people of good will can, and must, say the Rosary every day. Why? In order to put ourselves into contact with God, to thank Him for his benefits and ask Him for the graces we need. It is the prayer which places us in familiar contact with God like the son that goes to his father to thank him for the gifts he has received, to talk to him about his special concerns, to receive his guidance, his help, his support and his blessing.

Since we all need to pray, God asks of us, as a kind of daily installment, a prayer which is within our reach: the Rosary, which can be recited either in common or in private, either in Church in the presence of the Blessed Sacrament or at home, either with the rest of the family or alone, either when travelling or while walking quietly in the fields. A mother of a family can say the Rosary while she rocks her baby's cradle or does the housework. Our day has twenty four hours in it. It is not asking a great deal to set aside a quarter of an hour for the spiritual life, for our intimate and familiar converse with God.

On the other hand, I believe that, after the liturgical prayer of the Holy Sacrifice of the Mass, the praying of the Rosary, in view of the origin and sublime nature of the prayers used in it, and of the mysteries of the Redemption which we recall and on which we meditate during each decade, is the most pleasing prayer that we can offer to God, and one which is most advantageous to our own souls. If such were not the case, Our Lady would not have asked for it so insistently.

When I speak of saying the five or fifteen mysteries of the Rosary, I do not want to give the impression that God requires us to count the number of times that we address our supplications, our praise or our thanksgiving to Him. God certainly does not expect this of us: in Him everything is present! But we need to count, in order to have a clear and vivid idea of what we are doing, and to know positively whether or not we have completed what we had planned to offer to God each day, in order to preserve and enhance our relationship of intimacy with God and, by this means, preserve and enhance in ourselves our faith, hope and charity.

I would add that even those people who are able to assist at Mass every day should not, for this reason, neglect to say their daily Rosary. Obviously, the time they devote to saying the Rosary is not the same as that during which they are assisting at Mass. For such people, praying the Rosary can be looked upon as a way of preparing themselves to participate better in the Eucharist, or as an act of thanksgiving after it.

I don't know, but from the little knowledge that I have from my contact with people in general, I see that there are very few truly contemplative souls who preserve and maintain within themselves a relationship of intimate familiarity with God which prepares them for the worthy reception of Christ in the Eucharist. Thus, vocal prayer is necessary for them too, meditated, pondered and reflected upon as much as possible, as the Rosary should be.

There are many fine prayers that can be used as a means of preparing to receive Christ in the Eucharist, and of maintaining our intimate relationship with God. But I do not think that we shall find one more suited to people in general than the praying of the five or fifteen mysteries of the Rosary. For example, the prayer of the Liturgy of the Hours is marvellous, but I do not think it is accessible to all, nor that some of the psalms that one recites will be readily understood by all. It requires a certain degree of instruction and preparation which cannot be expected of all.

Perhaps for all these reasons, and others that we are unaware of, God, who is our Father and understands better than we do the needs of His children, chose to stoop to the simple ordinary level of all of us in asking for the daily recitation of the Rosary, in order to smooth for us the way to Him.

Finally, bearing in mind all that the Magisterium of the Church has said to us over the years about the praying of the Rosary – I shall remind you of some of these things further on – and what God, through the Message, has asked us for so insistently, we can conclude that the Rosary is the form of vocal prayer which is most suited to people in general, which we must appreciate, and which we must make every effort never to abandon. God and Our Lady know better than anyone else what is most appropriate for us and what we most need. Moreover, it will be a powerful means of helping us to preserve our faith, hope and charity.

Even for those people who do not know how, or who are not able to recollect themselves sufficiently to meditate, the simple act of taking the rosary in their hands in order to pray is already to become mindful of God, and the mention in each decade of a mystery of the life of Christ recalls Him to their minds; this in turn will light in their souls the gentle light of faith which supports the still smouldering wick, preventing it from extinguishing itself altogether.

On the other hand, those who give up saying the Rosary and who do not go to daily Mass, have nothing to sustain them, and so end up by losing themselves in the materialism of earthly life.

Thus the Rosary is the prayer which God, through his Church and Our Lady, has recommended most insistently to us all, as a road to and gateway of salvation: "Pray the Rosary every day" (Our Lady, 13th May 1917).

Ave Maria!

How to
Pray the
Rosary

Make the Sign of the Cross.

1. While holding the crucifix in the hand, recite the Apostles Creed.
2. On the first large bead, recite the Our Father.
3. On the three small beads, recite the Hail Mary for an increase of Faith, Hope, and Charity.
4. Recite the Glory Be to The Father.
5. Call to mind the first mystery and reflect upon it; then recite on the same large bead the Our Father.
6. On the ten small beads, recite the Hail Mary, keeping in mind the mystery.
7. Recite the Glory Be to the Father.
8. After each decade, "O My Jesus. . ."
9. When the fifth decade is completed, the Rosary is concluded with the Hail, Holy Queen.